MODERNIZING INDIAN AGRICULTURE IN 21st CENTURY
Challenges, Opportunities and Strategies

About the Editors

B.S. Hansra, Assistant Director General (Agri. Extn.) at the Indian Council of Agricultural Research, New Delhi had been Professor and Head; Department of Extension Education, Punjab Agricultural University, Ludhiana (Punjab). He taught UG and PG courses in extension education at P.A.U., Ludhiana for more than two decades and guided extension. programmes of the University. He has authored ten books and more than 180 research and popular papers. He has been awarded National Fellow Award during 1995 by the Indian Society of Extension Education. He is closely associated with many national and international professional societies.

G. Perumal, Director of Extension Education (Rtd.), did his Ph.D degree in Agricultural Extension from IARI, New Delhi 1975. He served in various capacities in the Tamil Nadu Agricultural University, Coimbatore, involving in Teaching, Research and Extension for almost four decades. During this period, he guided 30 M.Sc. (Ag.) and 20 Ph.D students in Agricultural Extension. Besides, he was able to bring out about 250 booklets, books, research and popular articles. He was consultant to GOI, UNDP and many other reputed organizations in the country. He was responsible for the initiation of the Society of Extension Education and also Founder Chairman of International Extension Fourm. He has retired on 1996. After his retirement, he formed a Trust to help rural children, farmers and others to uplift their life, in a small way—a small drop in the ocean.

K. Chandrakandan, former Director of Extension Education is presently working as Professor of Agriculture Extension at TNAU, Coimbatore (TN). He has experience of over three decades in the filed extension as well as university extension and research. He is teaching M. Sc. and Ph. D. courses in Extension Education He has guided more than 35 M. Sc., and Ph.D. students and published over 100 research papers and four books. He is a recipient of nine coveted awards and Gold Medals for Best Teacher (PG). Best Extension Research and Best Extension Worker. He has organised many National and International seminars and operated projects sponsored by SIDA, Sweden and IDRC, Canada. He is the Secretary and Vice-Chairman of the Society of Extension Education and International Extension Forum respectively. He is currently a member of Research Board of Advisors of American Biographical Institute International, U.S.A. Recently, he has been selected for the Fellow of Indian Society of Extension Education.

MODERNIZING INDIAN AGRICULTURE IN 21st CENTURY
Challenges, Opportunities and Strategies

Edited by
B.S. Hansra
G. Perumal
K. Chandrakandan

CONCEPT PUBLISHING COMPANY PVT. LTD.
NEW DELHI-110059

ISBN: 978-81-7022-905-6

First Edition 2001

Published and Printed by

Concept
Since 1974

Concept Publishing Company Pvt. Ltd.
A/15-16, Commercial Block, Mohan Garden,
New Delhi-110059 (India)
T: 91 11 41101460
E: publishing@conceptpub.com, *W*: www.conceptpub.com

FOREWORD

Agriculture in India occupies a pivotal position and contributes about one-third of our National Gross Product (GDP). The agricultural sector provides employment to nearly two-thirds of the workforce. India has successfully transformed situation of food deficit into that of self-sufficiency. We have had a record harvest of 209 million tonnes during 1999-2000 and our buffer stock of foodgrain figure has crossed an all time high of 45 million tonnes. These developments resulted in distinct gains in actual household food consumption leading to qualitative and quantitative improvement in our diet.

In the PAO World Food Summit held in 1990, Heads of different nations have reaffirmed, "the right of everyone to have access to safe and nutritious food, concerning with the right to adequate food and the fundamental right of everyone to be free of hunger". Also there was a pledge of political will and commitment, "to eradicate hunger in all countries, with an immediate view to reducing the number of under-nourished people by half their present level no later than 2015". We must, therefore, have a national commitment for a "Food Secure India" by 2015 and persue the goal through generating technologies that are globally competitive, environment friendly and conserve our natural resources.

Keeping this scenario in view, the International Extension Forum organized a National Symposium on "Modernising Indian Agriculture in 21st Century : Challenges, Opportunities and Strategies" during November, 2000. I am happy that the valuable inputs of participants, on all the major themes of the Symposium have been documented in this publication.

I congratulate Dr. B.S. Hansra and his colleagues for bringing out this timely publication which will be of use to policy makers, planners, administrators, researchers, extension scientists, students and all functionaries associated with the development of agriculture.

April 18, 2001

R.S. PARODA
Secretary, Department of Agricultural Research & Education
& Director General, Indian Council of Agricultural Research, New Delhi.

PREFACE

Indian agriculture has undergone several changes over the decades and centuries that have passed. Even in the last 50 years, since the time of Independence, a radical transformation has occurred in several facets of Indian agriculture due to planned interventions that has resulted in noteworthy economic progress. We have had a record production of 209 million tonnes of food grains during the year 2000 and our buffer stock figure has crossed all time high if 40 million tonnes. We have also become the largest producer of milk (76 million tonnes), and the second largest producer of rice (88.25 million tonnes), wheat (74.25 million tonnes), fruits (40 million tonnes) and vegetables (68 million tonnes) in the world. All these accomplishments could not have been possible but the sound technical backstopping provided by the National Agricultural Research System (NARS); Technology Assessment, Refinement and Dissemination System; and above all our farmers. It is they who had done the job.

During 1996 FAO World Food Summit all participating countries have reaffirmed the right of every individual to access to safe and nutritions food. The pledge was to eradicate hunger in all countries immediately by reducing number of undernourished and malnourished people by 2015. Therefore, India has to have a commitment for a "Food Secure India" by 2015. We have to double our food production in next decade. We have to generate technologies which are globally competitive, environment friendly and that conserve our natural resources.

Soil degradation, deforestation, water scarcity and contamination, bio-diversity loss and climate changes are increasingly at risk. Our soils are constantly being degraded and destroyed. It has become more hungry than thirsty. Water is another important threat for economic development. The water availability will decrease drastically which will adversely effect our capacity to produce more food.

It is expected that we shall need annually additional 5 million tonnes foodgrains besides oilseeds, fodder, fuelwood, fruits, vegetables, milk, meat, eggs, fish etc. All of these factors will have pressure to produce more food at a much accelerated pace. Serious imbalances also underlie the existing scenario.

India, having entered into WTO Agreement on Agriculture, has fully integrated itself with the world economy. The effect of this shift in Government policy from protected to liberalized economy is amply evident both at macro and micro level as reflected by declining share of primary and secondary sectors of Gross Domestic Product.

Of the major sectors of economy, the primary sector, which basically includes Agriculture, is most vulnerable to market forces. It is this sector which is going to undergo major changes.

Keeping in view these issues and challenges, International Extension Forum (IEF) organized a National Symposium on "Modernizing Indian Agriculture; challenges, opportunities and strategies" during 15-16 November, 2000 at Tamil Nadu Agricultural University, Coimbatore (TN). This book is based on the deliberations of the lectures and discussion of the participants.

The chapters in the book has divided under four main sub-headings: technology development, technology dissemination, technology utilization and strategies and policies. Besides these, few lead papers were also presented which have been included separately.

In first theme of technology development four chapters have been included. These papers mainly focused that participatory variety selection can be adopted for successful technological development and the participatory methodology will be ideal for early spread and acceptance of new varieties. Planning may be done as an area specific programme rather than a general programme in order to ensure cooperation of client system. Farmers need to be involved in all stages of operation of the project concerned for success of the programme. The concern was that human resource development should be given due importance in all the stages of technology development. Research system should address its research agenda according to the emerging needs of farming community and their economic states. Further indigenous technologies should be blended with remote sensing and information technology and such advancements for better development of agriculture.

The second theme was of technology dissemination in this 13 chapters have been included. In these chapters the authors have mainly analysed the emerging trends of privatization, scope of exploiting private and corporate services in extension. Pluralism in extension shall indeed mark the future of technology dissemination for meeting the ever changing needs. It was also emphasized that single window system be developed for proving information and services to the farmers in SAUs/ICAR Institutes. New concepts like cyber extension hold good promise and are likely to dominate the extension scenario in the future and also needs attention of the extension scientists.

The third part is on technology utilization. This section includes 8 chapters. The main issues in this unit are that small and marginal farmers should be organized to Self Help Groups (SHG) so that they can market their produce. The adoption of farm machinery has been far from satisfactory, efforts should be made that small tools and machinery are made available to the farmers on subsidized rates. This should be made available to group of farmers than the single farmer. Emphasis also need to be given to dry land technology for effective water harvesting, soil conservation, developing and maintaining common pastures and speedy implementation of the dry land agriculture project in the country.

In the last section of polices issues and recommendations chapters have been included. The major focus on genetic engineering for sustainable development and environmental protection needs of farmers should be kept in mind. Interactive demonstrations for dissemination of agricultural technologies should be one of the policies of the NARS.

The Vice-Chancellor, Tamil Nadu Agricultural University, Coimbatore (TN) gave lot of support and encouragement for which IEF and the authors are thankful. The pains taken by the Director of Extension Education and Dean, College of Agriculture of the University are praiseworthy.

The authors are indebted to Dr. R.S. Paroda, Secretary Department of Agriculture Research and Education and Director General, Indian Council of Agriculture Research for his encouragement and also for writing foreword of this book. The authors are also thankful to Dr. P. Das, Deputy Director General (Agricultural Extension) and past Chairman IEF for his continued support and guidance. Dr. A.G. Sawant, Member ASRB and Chairman IEF deserves special thanks for his guidance and help.

This book would not have been possible without the contributions from many scientists, students and organizations. We are thankful to all the authors of the chapters who had contributed on this theme with their best efforts and dedication. We are also thankful to Concept Publishing Company for helping in this venture.

B.S. HANSRA
G. PERUMAL
K. CHANDRAKANDHAN

CONTENTS

SECTION III : TECHNOLOGY DISSMINATION

SECTION IV : TECHNOLOGY UTILIZATION

LIST OF CONTRIBUTORS

Adhikari, Madhab, Department of Extension Education, Punjab Agricultural University, Ludhiana

Alauddin, A. Shaik, Associate Prof. PJN College of Agriculture and Research Institute

Anand Kumar, S., PJN College of Agriculture and Research Institute

Anandaraja, N., Department of Agricultural Extension, TNAU, Coimbatore (Tamil Nadu)

Annamalai, R., Tamil Nadu Agriculture University, Coimbatore

Arunachalam, P., Department of Plant Breeding and Genetics, COH, KAU, Vellamickare, Kerala

Balakrishnan, Nambiar Sajini, Department of Agricultural Economics, College of Horticulture, Kerala Agricultural University, Thrissur

Chandran, Rajula, Scientist (Sr. Scale) (Agricultural Extension) Sugarcane Breeding Institute, Coimbatore

Chandran, Rajula, Scientist, Surgercane Breeding Institute, Coimbatore

Choudhary, M.R., Prof. of Extension Education, College of Agriculture, Akda (MS)

Gowda, N.S. Shivalinge, Associate Prof. Department of Agricultural Extension, UAS, GKVK, Bangalore

Hansra, B.S., Assistant Director General Extension Education, ICAR, New Delhi

Jayachithra, N.K., Assistant Project Manager (Training), KHDP, Cochin

Jha, P.N., Ex-Vice-Chancellor, Dean, Agriculture, Rajendra Agricultural University, Pusa (Samastipur) Bihar (Indore)

Kalra, R.K., Department of Extension Education, COA, PAU, Ludhiana (Punjab)

Kannaigan, S., Vice-chancellor, Tamil Nadu Agricultural University, Coimbatore

Khare, N.K., Associate Prof. Department of Extension Education, JNKVU, Jabalpur

Krishnankutty, Jayasree, Department of Agriculture Extension, College of Horticulture, Kerala Agricultural University, Vellanikkara

Makhija, V.K., Department of Extension Education, COA, CCSHAU, Hissar

Moni, G.S., Prof. and Head, Department of Extension Education, Punjab Agricultural University, Ludhiana

Muthiah, Krishnaveni

Nehru, S. Motilal, Training Specialist, KHDP, Cochin

Panicker, Beena C., Post Gradute Student of College of Agriculture, Nagpur (MS)

Perumal, G., Former Director of Extension Education, TNAU and General Secretary, International Extension Forum

Philip, H., Deputy Director (Video), Directorate of Extension Education, TNAU, Coimbatore

Saravanan, R., Department of Agricultural Extension, GKVK, UAS, Bangalore (Karanataka)

Sawant, A.G., Chairman, Agricultural Scientist Recruitment Board, ICAR, Krishi Bhavan, Pusa, New Delhi-110012

Sawant, G.K., Department of Extension Education, Mahatma PhuleKrishi Vidyapeeth, Rahuri Dist. A., Nagar (MS), India

Seema, Tamil Nadu Agricultural University, Coimbatore

Sepastian, Shibu, Department of Agriculture Economics, College of Horticulture, Kerala Agricultural University, Vellanikkara, Thrissur

Selvaraj, C., Department of AE&RS, TNAU, Coimbatore

Selvaraj, G., Prof. Agricultural Extension, Tamil Nadu Agricultural University, Coimbatore

Shehrawat, P.S., Department of Extension Education, COA, CCSHAU, Hissar

Sherin, K.J., Department of Agricultural Extension, College of Horticulture, Kerala Agricultural University, Vellanikkara, Thrissur

Singh, Sube, Department of Extension Education, COA, CCSHAU, Hissar

Sriram, Research Associate, CCRI, Coimbatore

Swamiappan, M., Registrar, TNAU, Coimbatore

Swamy, B.K. Narayana, Prof. of Extension, Staff Training Units, Directorate of Extension, University of Agricultural Science, Hebbal, Bangalore

Theodore, Ravi Kumar, Asst. Prof. Agricultural Extension, Tamil Nadu Agricultural University, Coimbatore

Yelpanekar, P.H., Department of Extension Education, Mahatma PhuleKrishi Vidyapeeth, Rahuri Dist., A. Nagar (MS), India

SECTION I : LEAD PAPERS

1

AGRICULTURAL EXTENSION POLICY FROM FARMERS' PERSPECTIVE

— *A.G. Sawant*

PERSPECTIVE OF AGRICULTURAL EXTENSION

Agricultural Extension has been used by different countries vehicle to meet expanding demands for food and to cope with declining availability of land and water resources. It has served in various countries as a vehicle for encouraging technological changes in food and fibre production (Dinar, 1996). According to Farrington (1995), Extension conventionally comprises several of the following functions viz., (i) diagnosis of farmers' socio-economic and agro-ecological conditions and of their opportunities and constraints, (ii) message transfer through training courses and mass media and through direct contact between extension agent and farmer or indirect contact involving intermediaries such as contact farmers or voluntary organisations, (iii) feedback to researchers on farmers' reactions to new technology to refine future research agenda, and (iv) development of linkages with researchers, government planners, NGOs, farmers' organisations, banks and the private commercial sector. In remote areas, extension agents have taken on a number of input supply functions directly.

It goes without saying that the role performed by extension organisation vary from country to country. In United States, it has an educational task, whereas in European countries, Extension

Workers see their task as to helping farmers solve specific problems. In India and many other developing countries, extension task goes beyond that. It also deals with human resource development of its clients, teaching farmers the management and decision-making skills, helping rural people develop leadership and organisational skills, enabling them to organise better operate or participate in co-operative credit societies and other support organizations (Swanson and Clarr, 1984). A study on Indian Extension System conducted by the National Institute of Agricultural Extension Management (MANAGE, 1993) articulated that the public sector extension in India should embrace besides technology transfer, other roles like Human Resource Development, broad basing and farming systems perspective and gender strategies.

Agricultural Extension from farmers' perspective is a service provided by organizations (through its representatives/media) or individual experts who initiate activities that help them to make better decisions on matters related to their farming. Extension services could be from:

- department of the State/national government
- agricultural universities or a department or its wing providing advice/information
- input companies (seed/fertilizer/pesticide/farm machinery)
- non-governmental organizations
- agro-processors who provide technical support
- private consultants
- farmers' associations/co-operatives agricultural research stations
- mass media organisation (print/audio/video based)

In most of the countries, many of these organizations are present but their distribution and extension involvement vary considerably. A 113 country survey, conducted by the FAO in 1988-89 (Table 1.1) showed that national, State or provincial governments conducted approximately 81 per cent of the extension work in the surveyed countries. Based on the responses to the survey, universities, parastatals and non-governmental organisation comprised about 5 per cent (Swanson *et al.*, 1990).

Table 1.1 : Distribution of Extension Organisations based on FAO Survey of 113 countries.

No.	Types of organizations	Percentage
1.	National, State, provincial governments	81.0
2.	Non-governmental Organisations	7.0
3.	Parastatals	3.0
4.	Universities	2.0
5.	Private for profit sector	5.0
6.	Others	2.0
	Total	100.0

Source : Swanson *et al.*, 1990.

AGRICULTURAL EXTENSION SYSTEM WITH REFERENCE TO INDIA

There are four major pillars of the Indian extension or Transfer of Technology system: (i) agricultural extension service with the State governments, (ii) extension education system of ICAR and SAU system, (iii) extension programme of input industries in public and private sectors and NGOs, and (iv) special rural development programmes of the Central and State governments. However, main responsibility of transfer of technology rests with the State governments as agriculture is a State subject. The central government also implements several schemes having transfer of technology component, through the State governments.

The main extension system comprises the Directorate of Extension in the Ministry of agriculture at the centre and T&V system under the State Department of Agriculture. In the T&V system, professional extension workers work with contact farmers for the transfer of information and skill. Training support to the T&V system is provided by the ICAR/SAU system. The Directorate of Extension plans extension activities at national level and disseminates information through mass media and publication of literature. For training of extension staff, there is a three-tier training system. At the national level for training of senior and middle level staff, an autonomous institute, namely, National Institute of Agricultural Extension Management (MANAGE) was established. There are four regional extension training institutes and several State training institutes for training of extension workers. Several development programmes like integrated rural development programme, watershed development programme, operation flood, technology mission for crops etc. sponsored by other government departments contain transfer of technology component. In 1994, the scope of extension was widened under the 'broadbased agricultural extension' in farming system approach to include all landbased activities. The ICAR/SAU front-line extension system plays a catalytic and supportive role. It develops extension methodology, refines and transfers frontline technologies, and provides feedback to scientists. This system has three approaches. First is the special transfer of technology programmes like National Demonstration Programme (NDP), Operational Research Project (ORP) and Lab to Land Programme (LLP). Most recent in the series is the Institute-Village Linkage Programme started in 1995-96 for technology assessment and refinement. The second approach comprises the transfer of technology and training by the KVKs and TTCs on the principle of 'learning by doing'. There are 261 KVKs functioning in the country under the ICAR institutes, SAUs, NGOs, State Governments, Central Universities and Public Undertakings. Frontline extension programmes (ND, ORP, LLP) are presently merged with the KVKs. Eight TTCs provide training to the KVK staff. In the third approach, ICAR/SAU system provide training to the master trainers (subject matter specialists) working in the State line department through monthly workshops.

Private input companies are involved only in the transfer of chemical (fertilizers, pesticides), mechanical and biological (hybrid seeds) technologies developed/produced by them. Public sector companies and seed corporations also undertake transfer of technology activities related to the sale of their products i.e. farm inputs. Commodity groups/boards also promote commodity specific extension activities. Many NGOs also undertake extension activities as part of their development programmes. Some NGOs are also managing ICAR supported KVKs.

Trends on Extension Investment and Extension Intensity

Extension intensity increased from 0.09 per cent of AgGDP in the early 1960s to 0.14 per cent in the early 1970s, which further rose marginally to 0.15 per cent in the early 1990s after slight fall in the early 1980s. Annual investment in extension by governments during the triennium 1992-94, in nominal terms, is Rs.3008 million, giving an investment of Rs.16.22 per hectare. Annual expenditure per extension worker is 26 thousand for (average of all departments), whereas it is as low as Rs. 15 thousand for the main extension system, i.e. Department of Agriculture. Even making allowances for high proportion of low qualified extension workers (70 per cent of the total workers are intermediate or below, Misra, 1990), there are hardly any operational funds which are essential for mobility of extension workers. Macklin (1992) estimated that the share of non-salary component in total extension expenditure in Tamil Nadu decreased from 48 per cent in 1981/82 to 4 per cent in 1990/91.

Like research, private and public sector companies also undertake extension work to promote sales of their products, however, their extension expenditure data are not available. The private companies spend slightly higher amount on publicity and on an average they spend about 4 per cent of their turnover on research and 1 per cent on publicity. Private sector's participation in extension will grow alongwith the increase in its research investment and with the increase in farmer's ability to pay for extension services.

The growth in extension investment during the period 1974-75 to 1994-95 was negative in the high productivity States of Haryana and Punjab. These States were joined by the States of Karnataka, Kerala, Orissa and West Bengal during the period 1984-85 to 1994-95. In contrast the States of Uttar Pradesh, Tamil Nadu,

Jammu and Kashmir, Gujarat and Assam registered impressive growth in the investment during the second period. Although the nominal expenditure, production environment of other States needs higher level of extension efforts. Even in Punjab and Haryana, there is a need for intensive extension work as there would be greater role of crop and though resource per hectare increased in all States in the early nineties, it declined in real terms in the States of Haryana, Orissa, Punjab and West Bengal. The proportion of AgGDP spent on extension also declined in Bihar, Haryana, Karnataka, Kerala, Orissa and Punjab and this decline is serious because the intensity was already very low (0.06 per cent or less) in these States, except Bihar. Extension intensity in Himachal Pradesh and Tamil Nadu was more than twice of that for the country as a whole. These results, thus underline the need for increasing extension intensity in low productivity States, particularly in Andhra Pradesh, Kerala, Karnataka, Madhya Pradesh and Orissa.

The wide variations in extension intensity across the States are rather puzzling. These variations can partly be attributed to inter-State differences in the funding under the NAEP. Nevertheless, these differences need further discussion. For instance, the case of Punjab and Haryana is interesting in the sense that these States have high technology adoption levels, despite of very low extension intensity. The plausible reason could be the dominance of irrigated production environment in these States, which is conducive for rapid adoption of technology. Farmer-to-farmer spread of technology is much faster in the homogeneous, irrigated production environment. Moreover, these States have very high levels of inputs use, inviting greater attention of private input companies, which also undertake transfer of technology activities. Thus heterogeneous management technologies in these States and farmer-to-farmer spread of management technology are comparatively slow.

It is difficult to suggest some desired level of extension intensity. However, one can judge current extension intensity vis-a-vis the task ahead. Given current stock of technologies, there is tremendous scope for yield increase. It is estimated that excepting few States, there is untapped yield potential of 40 to 94 per cent in most important crops of the States (Jha *et al.*, 1995). This coupled with complexity of second generation technologies and heterogeneity of production environments warrant much more intensive extension efforts. Scaling up investment levels and improving the quality of extension should strengthen extension services. This is especially important for low extension intensity States like Andhra Pradesh, Kerala, Karnataka, Madhya Pradesh and Orissa.

FUTURE CHALLENGES

Food, nutrition environmental security are the major challenges in the context of increasing population. To keep pace the present trends, we need 5 million tonnes of additional foodgrains annually, besides significant increase in the production of livestock, fish and horticultural products. This has to be accomplished in the present scenario of declining total factor productivity growth, shrinking farm size, depleting natural resource base, increasing biotic and abiotic stresses and likely adverse impact of global climate change. Availability of energy and good quality water to meet the rising needs would be still crucial in future. Slow growth of employment in agriculture and industry threatens the income base and food security of the poor. Health and education deficiencies and gender inequities further restrict both income and employment opportunities. Declining capital investment and resource availability constraints development of physical and social infrastructure. The WTO and emerging IPR regime hinder the free flow of advanced technology and knowledge. Globalization of markets would influence domestic production and price stability. Trade prospects would also be influenced by the use of new kinds of barriers in the guise of food safety and social concerns.

RATIONALISED EXTENSION POLICY

In the context of meeting the holistic needs of increasing agricultural production yet do so in a sustainable manner, agricultural extension has a crucial role to play. Improvement in the system envisage an extension service more broad-based and holistic in content and scope, thus beyond transfer of technology. Its normal task of technology transfer would not be sufficient. Extension agencies, services and workers will need to exercise a more proactive and participatory role, serve as knowledge/information agents, initiating and facilitating mutually meaningful and equitable knowledge based transactions among agricultural researchers, trainers and primary producers. All this needs to be done in an effective and cost efficient manners with the long term objective of achieving financial sustainability.

Technology generation and its application will have to focus more strongly than before on the themes of optimization by producers of their available resources, sustainability, coping with diversity by adopting technology more specifically to agro-ecological or social circumstances. Creation of policy environment that promotes productive, profitable and sustainable farming.

Changes in agricultural extension have been initiated and proposed to be undertaken on wider scale are mentioned:

- Policy improvement
- Institutional restructuring
- Management refinement
- Strengthening Research – Extension Linkages
- Capacity building and skill upgradation
- Empowerment of farmers
- Mainstreaming of women in agriculture
- Use of Media and Information Technology

POLICY IMPROVEMENT

Farming Systems Approach

Policy improvement in agricultural Extension envisage the replacement of the old single-discipline based, commodity oriented approach of the T&V system by the Farming Systems (FS) approach. The FS approach considers the farm, the farm household and off farm activities in a holistic way to take care not only of farming but also all aspects of nutrition, food security, sustainability, risk minimization, income and employment generation which make up the multiple objectives of farm households. The FS approach emphasizes that research and extension agendas should be determined by explicitly defined farmers' needs through an understanding of the existing farming systems rather than its perceptions by research scientists or extension functionaries.

Multi-Agency Extension Service

For many years agricultural extension was considered the monopoly of the public sector. However, with the wide range of demands for agricultural technology in the changing scenario there is growing recognition that public extension by itself cannot meet the specific needs of various regions and different classes of farmers. The new extension regime recognises the role of a multi-agency dispensation comprised of different strengths. Policy environment will promote private and community driven extension to operate competitively, in roles that complement, supplement work in partnerships. The three arms of the agricultural extension network are:

PUBLIC EXTENSION SERVICES

- State government line departments operated extension (Departments of agriculture, Horticulture, Livestock development and other line departments).
- State agriculture universities based extension (Directorates of extension, Krishi Vigyan Kendras (KVK), Krishi Gyan Kendras (KGK), Farm Advisory Service etc.).
- ICAR frontline extension (Zonal Agricultural Research Stations/Krishi Vigyan Kendras, Agriculture Technology

Information Centre (ATIC) Institute Village Linkage Programme (IVLP)

PRIVATE EXTENSION SERVICES

- Community Based Organization (Farmers' Organizations, Farmers', Cooperatives, Self Help Groups)
- Para Extension Workers (contact farmers, para technicians, link farmers, gopals, mitra kisans, mahila mitra kisans)
- Input suppliers/Dealers (Pesticides, seeds, nutrients, farm implements)
- Corporate Sector (Commercial Crops – tobacco, tea, coffee, oilseeds (sunflower), vegetable seeds, Farm implements – tractors, threshers, sprinklers, drip irrigation)

MASS MEDIA AND INFORMATION TECHNOLOGY

- Print Media – Vernacular Press
- Radio, Television, Private Cable Channels.
- Electronic Connectivity through Computers, NICNET, Internet, V-SAT etc.
- Farmer Information Advisory Centres (FIAC)
- Public and Private Information Shops

Public Extension Services

Despite the rise of the private sector in the provision of agro-services such extension will gravitate towards selected regions, crops and sectors where gains are to be appropriated. Pure public goods, economically backward regions, small, marginal farmers and landless labourers will not attract for profit the private sector. Public Extension will therefore continue to play a central role in technology dissemination. For example, public extension should focus its efforts on those knowledge based technologies that are central to farmers concerns and that will maintain the natural resource base. These are subject matter areas that are not likely to be taken by the private sector. Examples include dissemination of production management technologies that are specific to different crops and livestock systems; natural resource management technologies, such as soil and water management, integrated pest management, agro-forestry and other technologies associated with sustainable development and farming systems technologies, including farm management skills that will enable farmers to improve their efficiency, increase cropping intensities and to diversify into more high value commodities.

Promotion of Farmer Participatory Approach

There is, therefore, a need of more farmers' participatory approach in working out the system description, problem diagnosis, search for appropriate technology, designing the process of implementation, monitoring and evaluation and feedback. The extension agent is no longer seen as the expert who has all the useful information and technical solutions; the indigenous technical knowledge of farmers knowledge and their ingenuity, individually and collectively are recognized as a major source; solution to local problems are to be developed in partnership between the extension agent and farmers. Extension workers therefore need new skills of negotiations, conflict resolution and mobilizing and nurturing community organizations.

Promotion of Demand-driven and Farmer Accountable Extension

Under the T&V system, the technology dissemination regime was more supply driven. Research and extension agendas were pre-set based on technologies for high yielding varieties of wheat and rice. An important reason why research and extension organisations have not focused on farmer problems is due to the lack of an effective feedback system. The vast majority of small and marginal farmers in India, especially women, lack an effective voice in influencing research and extension priorities. Under the new policy agenda a demand driven extension system need be created by providing farmers with access to linkage mechanisms through which they can articulate their problems and needs. A key factor in improving these feedback systems is to organise farmers into functional groups, such as Self Help Groups (SHGs), farmer interest groups (FIGs), Commodity Associations (CAs) and/or other types of Farmer Organization (FOs). These FOs can provide an effective channel for both the dissemination of technology to large numbers of small and marginal farmers and they can provide an effective feedback channel to research and extension. Meaningful farmer representation in the governing bodies of public and private extension services. Farmer influence on decisions on the planning, implementation and monitoring of public extension at local, regional and national levels. Farmer influence on the incentives of extension staff, including supervisors and subject matter specialists.

Institutional Restructuring

It is clear that no one uniform extension system will serve as a remedy to all States. Even within States there will be a combination of various agencies and different institutional arrangements to address needs of differing agroclimatic zones as well as different sections of farmers. A menu of various models will be available to the States to select and adapt to their own requirements.

Restructuring Public Extension

It will continue to remain central to technology dissemination, small and marginal farmers and economically backward regions will need to be serviced by it. This implies that the 1,00,000 public extension functionaries (including VEWs and SMSs) will have to be placed in new decentralized institutional arrangements which are demand-driven, farmer accountable, bottom up and have a Farming Systems Approach (broad based). States have before them several models. Namely, (i) the ATMA model (6 States) (ii) Single Window – broad based extension Model (Maharashtra), Panchayati Raj Institutions

(Kerala, W.B., M.P.) and the SAU Farmer Direct Contact (Punjab).

Agricultural Technology Management Agency (ATMA) Model

A key concept is to decentralise decision-making to the district level through the creation of the ATMA as a registered society. A second goal is to increase farmer input into programme planning and resource allocation, especially at the block level and to increase accountability to stakeholders. A third major goal is to increase programme coordination and integration between departments so that the following programme thrusts can be more effectively and efficiently implemented.

- (i) *Farming System Innovations* : especially the intensification and/or diversification into high value commodities and/or value added marketing and processing activities,
- (ii) *Farmer Organizations* : especially for high value commodities and resource poor farmers,
- (iii) Technology Gaps in both crop and livestock production systems, and
- (iv) *Natural Resource Management* : especially soil and water management and to reduce pesticide use through integrated pest management (IPM) programmes.

Strategic Research and Extension Plans (SREPs) through Participatory Rural Appraisal (PRA)

In the process of creating a more bottom-up extension system PRA procedures would be introduced across all system levels (district, block, mandal and village) and across each participating line department (DOA, DOH and DAH) and research institution (ZRS and KVK) within the district. On the basis of PRA, Strategic Research Extension Plans would be prepared for the districts. The district SREP must be grounded at the block or mandal level, where extension programmes can be fine-tuned to the needs of farmers and more effectively implemented.

Block/Mandal Level Technology Centre for Single Window Extension System. Concept of a Block (or Mandal) Technology Centre (BTC) has emerged wherein a multidisciplinary technology team (comprising of block level agriculture, horticulture, soil and water conservation and livestock extension officers) would be assigned to organise and implement extension programmes within the block. Other line department units and personnel would continue to provide essential service and developmental activities. In effect, the BTC would result in the functional integration of extension activities within the block or mandal and in effect become the operational arm of the ATMA. This Centre would become the common meeting point for extension personnel from the line departments to prepare integrated work plans (WPs) and to coordinate their implementation. It would also be the level where farmer input could be more effectively mobilised through a single Farmer Advisory Committee (FAC). The President of the elected Panchayat Agricultural Committee would chair the FAC that would include 10-12 members representing all major stakeholders within the block. The FAC would help set block extension priorities and recommend resource allocation across programme areas. The block technology team would be responsible for operationalizing the SREP in each block and moving towards a single window extension system.

Review of ICAR Role in Extension

The primary mandate of ICAR is research. Its extension programmes should be limited to reinforcing the research activities to make them more demand driven and farmer centric. At present, the extension activities through 261 KVKs are drawing away about 10 per cent of the ICAR Plan funds. This is likely to increase further as the ICAR strives to establish one KVK in every district by the end of the Ninth Plan. Efforts were made towards the end of the Eighth Plan to transfer the financial and administrative responsibilities of KVKs to their respective State Governments, which could not materialize because of the severe resource constraints faced by the States. Hence, Krishi Vigyan Kendras would continue to operate in pro-active mode, retaining their allegiance with ICAR for project implementation activities.

MANAGEMENT REFINEMENT

Under the present arrangement, mainstreaming of KVKs with the State extension mechanisms has been weak. KVKs set up as centres for location specific, adaptive research if effectively organised to achieve their primary objective of refinement and validation of local technologies could play a strategic role in linking the research and extension systems particularly in the area of farming systems based technologies. It is, therefore, imperative that KVKs as district level technology refinement institutions are integrated with the extension machinery is demonstrated rather than as just another vocational training organization which they are largely perceived as at present and of which there are several others at the district level. Hence, Krishi Vigyan Kendras would continue to operate in pro-active mode, retaining their allegiance with ICAR, for project implementation activities.

IMPROVING RESEARCH-EXTENSION LINKAGES

Promotion of Direct Interface between Farmers and Scientists

The direct interface between scientists and farmers is the most ideal and should be undertaken wherever possible. It is an oft repeated refrain that farmers learn best from scientists or other successful farmers. Moreover, transmission losses are minimized in the direct interface. However, there are relatively high costs attached to this direct mode of technology transfer and the outreach of scientists is limited. Punjab agriculture University has achieved significant success through this system. It must be noted however, that Punjab is geographically a small State and what is applicable to Punjab may not be possible in large States such as Uttar

Pradesh, Madhya Pradesh and Maharashtra.

CAPACITY BUILDING OF EXTENSION FUNCTIONARIES

Formulation of Training Plan for Extension Functionaries

A long-term training plan should be developed by each State based on a thorough skill gap analysis. A massive campaign for skill upgradation and capacity building of extension functionaries using resources of all training institutes. The training be divided into Foundation Courses comprising of skill upgradation in (i) need assessment techniques including the role of participatory rural appraisal, (ii) group formation, (iii) development of leadership skills, (iv) conflict resolution and negotiations between different interest groups, (v) management of common property resources, (vi) use of different types of media, (vii) communication, (viii) project preparation, (ix) data collection analysis and documentation. Foundation courses should be conducted jointly with scientists of SAUs. Professional courses would be conducted at SAUs and Centres of Excellence at the ICAR Institutes in various subject matter disciplines.

Networking among all State level institutes. All national and State level training institutes will be networked to State headquarters, SAUs and MANAGE.

EMPOWERMENT OF FARMERS

Involving Farmers in Setting Extension Agendas

Representation of farmer/senior citizens with working experience in agriculture and allied fields as major stakeholders will be ensured in all decision making bodies of public and private extension services. There will be involved in the planning and implementation of extension programmes through formal institutional mechanisms such as ATMAs, FACs etc..

Implementation of Programmes through Farmers' User Groups

Through ensuring that all programmes in the field are planned and implemented through farmer user groups such as Watershed association, fruit/vegetable growers cooperatives/societies etc. farmers would be able to influence both administrative and financial decision. Contracting arrangements between governments, extension services and farmers, whereby the farmers could play the role of purchaser, provider or co-financier of extension services.

MAINSTREAMING WOMEN IN AGRICULTURE

Gender concerns need to be mainstreamed in the agricultural extension process. Public extension systems which must disseminate new technology and information are still largely male dominated. Hence, the necessity to target women to ensure they receive information relevant to their work with crop and livestocks.

USE OF INFORMATION TECHNOLOGY

Information Technology revolution is unfolding and has very high visibility. However, its benefits have remained confined primarily to the urban areas. Rural communities, have not been able to gain to the same extent from IT. As a means of agricultural technology transfer to farmers, information technology, has had a limited impact. Even the vast potential of the broadcasting network has been tapped only minimally for extension.

CONCLUSION

We envision poverty, hunger and malnutrition free and environmentally safe India by 2020. It could be achieved through rapid economic growth by harnessing modern science blended with indigenous knowledge, wisdom and unique socio-cultural ethos. It is believed India will emerge as a developed nation by banishing poverty and promoting growth through sustainable use of our human, natural and other resources. In this context, from farmers perspective rationalised agricultural Extension system envisage an Extension service more broadbased and holistic in content and scope. It seeks promotion of farmer participation approach in working out the system description, problem diagnosis, search for appropriate technology, process of implementation, monitoring and evaluation and feedback as the indigenous technical knowledge of the farmers and their ingenuity, solution of local problems are to be developed in partnership between the Extension agents and the farmers. Extension mechanism therefore will have to be driven by farmers' meets, be location specific and addressed diversification demand. There is room for both public and private sector in the development of demand based and feedback driven system.

REFERENCES

Anonymous (2000). Vision 2020 and Strategic Action Plan of Agriculture, Ministry of Agriculture, Government of India, New Delhi.

Dinar, A. (1996). Extension Commercialisation: How Much to Charge for Extension Services. *American Journal of Agricultural Economics*. Vol.78, pp.1-12.

Farrington, J. (1995). The Changing Public Role in Agricultural Extension. *Food Policy*. 20(6) pp. 537-544.

MANAGE (1993). *Farmers Participation in Agricultural Research and Extension Systems*, Concept Publishing Company, New Delhi.

Pal, S. and Singh, A. (1997). Agricultural Research and Extension in India : Institutional Structure and Investment. Policy Paper 7, National Centre for Agricultural Economic Policy Research, New Delhi.

Sulaiman, V.R. and Sadamate, V.V. (2000). Privatising Agricultural Extension in India, Policy Paper 10, National Centre for Agricultural Economic Policy Research, New Delhi.

Swanson, B.E. and Clarr, J.B. (1984). *Agricultural Extension – a Reference Manual*, 2nd Edition, FAO, Rome.

2

MODERNIZATION OF INDIAN AGRICULTURE IN THE 21st CENTURY : Reforms in Technology Development and Technology Dissemination

— *S. Kannaiyan*

According to the Oxford English Dictionary, 'Modernization' refers to the action or an act of modernizing; the state of being modernized. The International Encyclopaedia of Social Sciences (1972) explains modernization as the current term for an old process – the process of social change whereby less developed societies acquire characteristics common to more developed societies. However, the concept of modernization is a relative term or a measure that cannot be stated in absolute terms. What is modern now may not be considered modern tomorrow. What is modern for one country may not be modern for the other. In the context of modernization, the agricultural development process could be designated either as modern or traditional by means of certain specific indicators. Table 2.1 outlines certain important indicators that differentiate a modern from a traditional kind of agricultural development.

Indicators of Modern Agriculture

At present, peasant agriculture in India is well suited to

modernization, and peasant farmers are already reacting in an economically rational way to their environment. What is needed to bring about decisions that will increase production and incomes is to change the environment within which peasant farmers make decisions.

Table 2.1: Indicators of Modern and Traditional Agriculture

S.No.	Indicators	
	Modern	Traditional
1.	Market economy	Protected economy
2.	Export oriented	Import oriented
3.	Commercialization, Agri business and Enterpreneurship	Subsistence farming/non-market oriented
4.	Sustainable Agriculture	Exploitative Agriculture
5.	Farm diversification	Monoculture and Crop specialisation
6.	Biotechnology and Transgenics for crop improvement	Natural selection and propagation through seed
7.	Use of Biofertilizers, Biopesticides and Biocontrol	Use of Inorganic fertilizers and Chemical pesticides
8.	Value addition	Ignorance of post harvest processing and value addition
9.	Organised into self-help groups and user groups	Individualistic and unorganised
10.	Women's empowerment and emancipation	Male dominated
11.	Cyber/Computer regime	Radio and Print regime

Achievements

Indian agriculture has undergone several changes over the decades and centuries that have passed. Even in the last 50 years, since the time of Indian Independence, a radical transformation has occurred in several facets of Indian agriculture due to planned interventions that has resulted in noteworthy economic progress. The highlights of achievements in the agricultural sector are listed below.

- Indian agriculture contributes 30-35 per cent of Gross Domestic Product (GDP) of the country and generates about 20 per cent of export earnings.
- The irrigated area has increased from 22.6 ha during 1950-51 to 89.42 million hectares (mha) during 1995-96, which is 23.60 per cent of the world irrigated area. India is rated as number two in the world for irrigation potential.
- Foodgrain production increased form a low level of about 72 million tonnes (mt) in 1965-66 to an impressive level of about 205 mt in 1999-2000, a growth of little over 2.5 per cent per annum.
- Buffer stock, which was just 2.2 mt in 1965-66, rose to more than 30 mt in recent years.
- Rice production reached a new height in 1998-99 with production touching 84.74 mt. Wheat production also set a new record with 71.01 mt. Total Pulses production rose to 15.89 mt, which is first in the world and oil seed production reached around 26 mt and potato production reached around 25 mt. Tea production (0.79 mt) ranks first in the world. India ranks second in the world with respect to Sugarcane production with 290 mt. Cotton also did well with production upto 127.7 lakh bales (third in the world). Fruits production reached around 50 mt and vegetable production reached around 80 mt. Milk has gone upto 74 mt and fish 5.38 mt.
- Marketing has been revolutionized by establishing Farmer Markets (Uzhavar Shandies) in several places of each district.

Challenges

India cannot dare to remain complacent with the success achieved so far in agricultural sector. Much more needs to be done. Indian agriculture continues to face several problems, challenges and threats that are obstacles in the way to rapid progress. Some of the important challenges are presented as follows:

India's population is projected to be around 135 million by 2025

AD, which will require additional production of foodgrain. Considering the current foodgrain production levels, India has a compulsive need to raise foodgrain production by 5 mt per year as against 3.1 per year achieved over the past 40 years. It has been estimated that the realistic demand for foodgrains is at 197 mt for the year 2000, which has been achieved by recording 205mt, 232-235 mt for 2015 and 260-264 mt by 2030. According to a recent study, in 2030 the domestic demand will be about 114 mt for rice, 80-83 mt for wheat, 13 mt for maize and 24-26 mt for pulses. Production of cereals, pulses and oilseeds have to grow at the rate of 3.5, 4.0 and 4.5 per cent respectively from the present growth rate of 2 to 2.5 per cent per annum. In 2000, the demand for milk is estimated at 77- 82 mt, vegetables around 84 mt, fruits around 50 mt, meat around 5.5 mt, eggs around 2 mt and fish around 6 mt, whereas in 2030, the demand is likely to be 130-158 mt (milk), 151-193 mt (vegetables), 84-106 mt (fruits), 10-14 mt (meat), 3.6-4.8 mt (eggs) and 10-14 mt (fish).

About 67 per cent of the country's arable land is rainfed, contributing 44 per cent of the foodgrains and supporting 40 per cent of the population. These regions are also home for two-thirds of the livestock population in the country. Droughts and crop failures are quite common in these rainfed areas. Usually, a single short duration crop is grown. It is characterized by resource-poor small and marginal farmers, poor infrastructure and low investments in technology and inputs. The average productivity in rainfed systems is only 0.7 to 0.8 tonnes per ha. More than 70 per cent of India's agriculture is under small and marginal farmers with limited resources. The per capita land availability of land is 0.60 ha, one of the lowest in the world. Sub-division and fragmentation of holdings have increased. The average size of farm holdings is 1.82 ha, but is fragmented into 5-6 smaller units reducing the operating unit to 0.3 to 0.4 ha only.

There lies a huge gap between actual yields and the potential. According to a rough estimate, India has over one hundred thousand paid agricultural extension personnel and about 30,000 agricultural scientists. In spite of these facts, only 30-40 per cent of the innovations is being adopted by the farmers.

Illiteracy rate is also high in India –52 per cent, as against less than 5 per cent in developed countries. There is prevalence of chronic unemployment and under-employment in the country. Roughly 25 to 40 per cent of the population in India suffers from malnutrition. In 1990 the average calorie intake of food was only 2,229 as, compared to over 3,400 calories per day in most of the developed countries. This is slightly above the minimum intake for sustaining life estimated at 1,800 calories.

Out of the total geographical area of 329 mha, 175 mha (53.0 per cent) of land is affected by land degradation. It has been estimated that about 12 billion tonnes of soil is eroded annually in the country. According to Rao (1997) there is concern about sustainability of one of the most productive cropping systems viz., rice-wheat, covering around 10 mha. It has been estimated that India contributes about six per cent of the global methane (green house gas) budget due to rice cultivation.

Standards for Modernization

Standards or success criteria help us to evaluate the progress made in the process of modernization of Indian agriculture with specific standards. The National Policy on Agriculture seeks to actualise the vast untapped growth potential of Indian Agriculture with specific standards. Over the next decades, it aims at: a growth rate in excess of four per cent per annum in the agriculture sector; growth that is based on efficient use of resources and conserves our soil, water and bio-diversity; growth with equity i.e., growth which is widespread across regions and farmers; growth that is demand driven and caters to domestic markets and maximizes benefits from exports of agricultural products in the face of challenges arising from economic liberalization and globalization; growth that is sustainable technologically, environmentally and economically.

Modernization of Indian Agriculture

"It would be an unsound fancy to expect that things

which have never yet been done can be done except by methods which have never been tried"

– *Sir Francis Bacon*

The ultimate goal of modernizing Indian agriculture would be to achieve sustainable agriculture. The process of modernization involves identifying the appropriate subject matter areas and suggesting suitable technology interventions. In the process of development we should not lose sight of the various concerns confronting the agricultural sector, which influence the modernization process. The concerns are ecological agriculture, globalisation, irrigated *vs.* rainfed agriculture, size of farm holdings and agricultural labourers. Further, the concept of modernization to reach the farmers and others concerned, the extension system needs to be revamped with farmer oriented approaches, gradual privatisation of the services and use of cyber extension. The paradigm of modernization of Indian agriculture is depicted in Figure 2.1.

Thrust Areas with Technology Interventions

The following are the key thrust areas that would help the modernization process to a greater extent. Appropriate technology interventions to be made under each area is also suggested to develop cutting-edge technologies.

Hybrid Rice

India needs to increase rice production by two mt every year to sustain the present self sufficiency. Hybrid rice technology is an innovative technology, which can solve this problem. The potential of hybrid rice is that it can produce 15 to 20 per cent more grain than the highest yielding check variety. The strategy to popularise hybrid rice technology would be to increase the magnitude of heterosis by developing the two line hybrids and developing inter sub-specific Indica/tropical Japonica hybrids; developing rice hybrids possessing resistance to major pests and diseases; improving

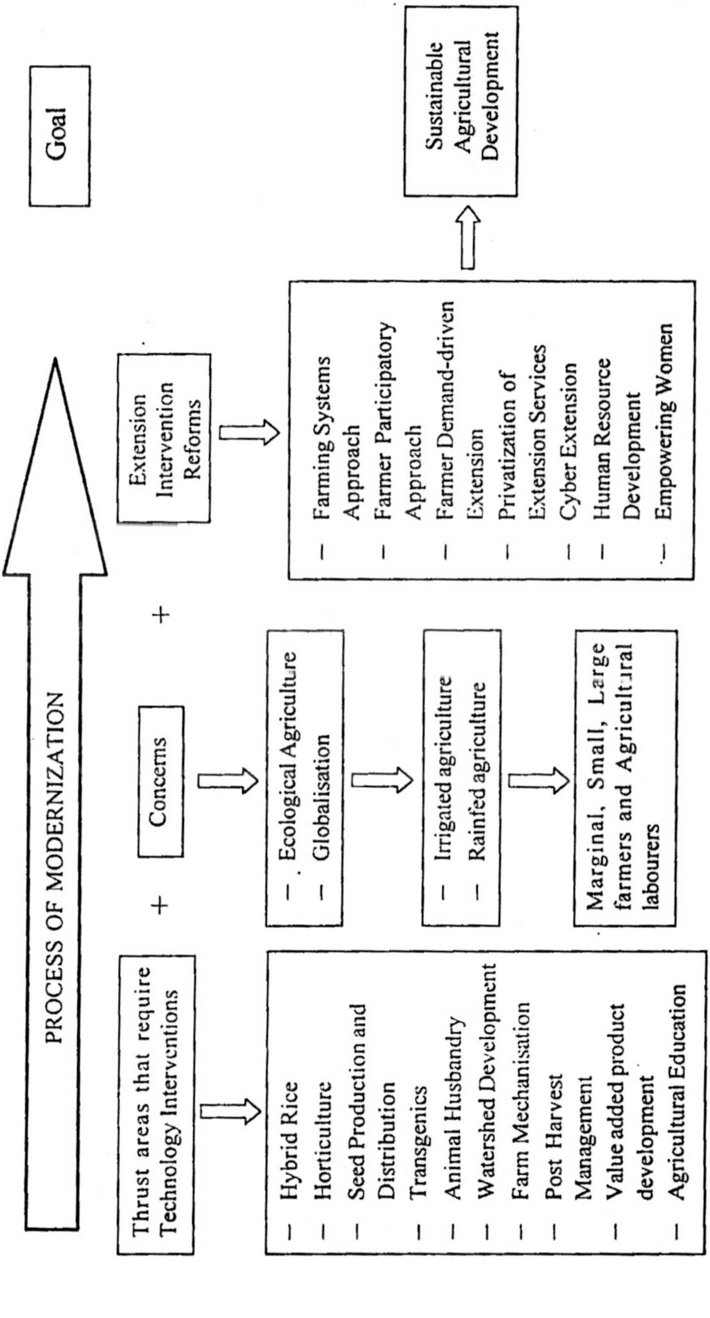

Fig 2.1 : Paradigm for Modernization of Indian Agriculture

seed production technology and better agronomic management practices in seed production plots to obtain seed yields beyond two tonnes per hectare; improving grain quality for consumer acceptance and; introducing a system of registration of parental lines for free exchange of parental lines between public research institutions and private seed agencies. The grain quality and pest(s) and disease(s) resistant Hybrid rice varieties are essentially required for Indian farmers. Hybrid rice would increase the yield per unit area i.e. 8-10 t/ha average yield. The Hybrid seed production in seed village concept should be encouraged (Kannaiyan, 2000).

Horticulture

Horticultural crops cover 6.1 per cent of the cultivable area and contribute 25 per cent of the total agricultural exports of the country. India stands second in terms of production of fruits and vegetables in the world. In order to be globally competitive, development of transgenics resistant to biotic and abiotic stresses; development of F1 vegetable hybrids for high yield, nutrition and export; development of horticultural crop-based cropping systems for different agro-climatic zones; standardisation of micro-irrigation and fertigation; standardisation of package of practices for protected cultivation of vegetables and flowers; micro-propagation of mango, guava and sapota; development of resistance free IPM using eco-friendly components like biological control agents, botanicals, pheromones and trap crops and; standardisation of technologies for extending shelf-life of cut flowers.

Seed Production and Distribution

Bradford and Cohn (1998) stated that "Seeds are the connection between the past and the future. They contain the accumulated genetic materials of the past, and the potential for its perpetuation in the future". One of the specialised agricultural sectors that emerged, tightly coupled with emergence of commerce and trade, have been the seed production and distribution. Seed production, quality and marketing have become highly important in the present agricultural scenario, particularly with the advent of hybrid breeding. To meet the seed demand seed village concept can be adopted. By this method, a particular variety of seed can be produced in the whole village area, which also solves the problem of isolation and genetic purity. This will also assure availability of adequate quantity of desired seed material in the local areas.

Transgenics

Transgenic technology is an emerging technology, which would dramatically change the genetic potential of crops. It is an important tool in our current agricultural system in meeting the future challenges of feeding an ever-increasing population. At present, the prominent traits that are particularly targeted through genetic engineering for development of transgenic crops worldwide are herbicide tolerance, pest(s) resistance, product quality and viral resistance (James, 1998). In India several transgenic lines are under advanced stages of development and also under field-testing. The major challenge in the coming years will be – how to effectively blend this technology with the traditional means of crop breeding in an environmentally sustainable manner and; how to generate awareness among farmers and consumers about this powerful technology. Genetic engineering in crop plants would decide the future of many developing countries in the world to meet the food requirements. Genetically modified crops are going to rule in the world. Certain groups claim themselves as environmentalists in the Western World and also similar lobbies are also emerging in developing countries including India without understanding the basic fundamentals of biotechnology issues. These groups and lobbies also should understand critical biosafety mechanisms available before releasing a transgenic crop. Transgenic crops with desired aminoacids or vitamins is important for eliminating the malnutrition among poor people.

Animal Husbandry

The increasing human population and improving per capita income are expected to boost demand for livestock products substantially. Though the country possesses one-fifth of the world's bovine population, it contributes only around eight per cent of the world's milk production, mainly due to the low productivity of animals. It has been reported through nutritional studies that milk production could be increased by 20 to 30 per cent by improved feeding. Enrichment of low quality feeds through pre-treatments and exploiting non-conventional feed sources are the measures that could be suggested for improving feed and fodder situation in the country. Many of the livestock services are only public, being delivered by the Government Veterinary Department. Due to fiscal constraints it leads to a decline in the operational efficiency of public livestock services. The mandate of the Government with regard to livestock services should be modified in such a way that the current veterinary services and artificial breeding be moved to private hands and Government devotes their energy on disease prevention and control.

Watershed Development

The Watershed approach aims at augmentation and stabilization of production and productivity, minimising ecological degradation, reduction in regional disparity, opening up of greater opportunities for employment of rural poor in the rainfed areas. A 25-year perspective plan for holistic and integrated development of rainfed areas, prepared by the Planning Commission, envisages treatment of about 63 mha of land involving an estimated outlay of Rs.76,000 crores through various watershed development projects. The strategy involves participatory approach for empowerment of the village community and implementation of the watershed project. For the strategy to be successful, it requires people's cooperation among the different castes and classes; able local leaders to guide and motivate the people; ability to resolve conflicts on a win-win basis and; the will to sustain the development even after the project period is over.

Farm Mechanisation

Mechanisation stands for modernization. During the last 30 years, the demand for agricultural machinery has increased substantially and has reached a level of Rs.30,000 crores annually. The increased demand for foodgrains in the coming years, calls for greater engineering inputs. The major thrust would be mechanisation of small farmers and dryland agriculture; conservation tillage to minimize energy, reduce turn around time between two crops and make efficient utilisation of available soil moisture; development of equipment to be used by farm women; mechanisation of horticultural crops; and use of micro-chip computer aided irrigation system.

Post-Harvest Management

As on date, we are processing only less than two per cent of our farm produce and convert only seven per cent of them as value added products. More than Rs. 50,000 crores of money is lost every year due to post-harvest losses. The future thrust areas would be development of appropriate drying and dehydration equipment for field crops, horticultural crops and fisheries to minimise losses, their handling, safe storage and transport; cold chambers and cold chains for perishable commodities; processes and equipment for value added products; processing of agricultural, horticultural, animal and fisheries products for export; development and popularisation of agro-processing models and; processing and utilisation of agricultural byproducts.

Agricultural Education

Education is an investment for prosperity. There are presently 31 Agricultural Universities in the country, which are basically meant for development of the agricultural economy. According to Paroda

(1998), the agricultural education in the country is stagnating and has started showing signs of decline in quality in recent years. So much so, the indicators are increasing numbers of agricultural graduates being unemployed and underemployed and; lack of confidence to self-employment activities. To reverse this trend and to develop employable agricultural graduates reforms in curricula have to be brought about such as giving priority to Rural Agricultural Work Experience, increasing the number of commercial courses and focus on agri-business management. Experiential learning system is being adopted in Rural Agricultural Work Experience in TNAU and RAWE programme is shifted from final year Agriculture students to second year students. This minor shift of the RAWE course to second year students have dramatically changed the learning process and infused confidence among students (Kannaiyan, 1999). The Tamil Nadu Agricultural University has taken a lead in this direction to vitalise the quality of agricultural education.

Concerns in the Process of Modernization

The following concerns should be taken into consideration while planning for modernizing agriculture since, they would greatly influence the modernization process:

Ecological Agriculture

A new paradigm of agricultural research and development is needed for enduring global and national food security involving development and use of environmentally friendly science and technology such as biotechnology, renewable energy, establishing high diversity, low external input agriculture, agro-forestry, and integrated pest and nutrient management. Basically, unsustainability in development stems from a lack of reconciliation between Nature economy and Market economy. The latter is based on production, capital, labour and resources. Gross National Product (GNP) as an index of development is questionable. The natural resources are not free gift of nature and have to be costed properly.

Depreciation in these has also to be properly, accounted for, as is always done in the case for manmade assets. For instance, soil is an extremely vital resource. Loss of soil *per se* and loss in its fertility are to be accounted for in future accounting system. The basic question is to have a correct price tag for natural resources. It is something that we must work out at the earliest. True economic growth equals growth in GNP (which must also include the value of Gross National Natural Resource Product) minus the cost of short and long term ecological costs.

Globalisation

India's signing of GATT agreement in 1994 and joining of WTO as founder member has put her agriculture into framework of global competition and the rule of global market. Gains for India will mostly depend on two factors: Whether she is a net exporter or importer of the commodities whose prices in the world market are expected to go up; and whether over period of time, it can generate adequate exportable surplus in some of these commodities at competitive rates.

The impact of Intellectual Property Rights (IPRs) on agricultural sector is an important dimension of analysis. Genetically engineered varieties of seed owned by multinational companies will be sold in India and such seeds will have royalty, which have so far been absent. This will increase the seed price and farmers may not be allowed to save the seeds from their own harvest. The multinationals would control the entire range of seed, fertilizers, pesticides and research, besides have a command on investment, production, distribution and marketing. The worst sufferers will be small and marginal farmers. Continuous effort is needed to minimize the damages and maximize the benefits by upgrading the agricultural technology; working out ways to protect the rights of plant breeders, the producers and the export companies in the seed trade; devise mechanisms to protect the interests of small and marginal farmers; formulating means to protect biodiversity as well as our indigenous knowledge system and; creating awareness about intellectual property rights in the country.

The other concerns viz., irrigated *vs.* rainfed agriculture, size of holdings and landless agricultural labourers should be taken into consideration in the process of modernization.

Extension Intervention Reforms

Public sector extension has undergone several changes since independence, beginning with the Community Development Programme in 1952 through the National Extension Service in 1953, the Intensive Agriculture District Programme started in 1961-62, the Intensive Agriculture Area Programme in 1964-65, the High Yielding Varieties Programme in 1966-67, and the Small and Marginal Farmers Development Programme initiated in 1969-70. The most significant recent development was the introduction of the Training and Visit (T&V) system, starting in the mid 1970s. The T&V system profoundly influenced practices and registered impressive gains in irrigated areas but failed to create an impact in rainfed areas. The T&V system was a top-down approach which generated uniformity rather than specificity and has lacked focus on location specific needs of regions, disadvantaged areas, target groups, enterprises etc. Linkages between research-extension and farmer remained weak.

By the early 1990's it was recognized that extension should broadbase its programmes, by utilizing a Farming Systems Approach. Attention should be given to diversifying extension programmes into livestock, horticulture and other value-based commodities that would increase farm incomes. Present day agriculture defined by key concepts of stability, sustainability, diversification and commercialisation there is need for reorientation of the philosophy of extension from technology transfer mode to technology application. The reforms in agricultural extension required to be undertaken are as follows:

Farming Systems Approach

Farming Systems (FS) Approach considers the farm, the farm household and off farm activities in a holistic way to take care of not only farming but also all aspects of nutrition, food security, sustainability, risk minimisation, income and employment generation which make up the multiple objectives of farm households. The FS approach emphasizes that research and extension agendas should be determined by explicitly defined farmers' needs through an understanding of the existing farming systems rather than its perceptions by research scientists or extension functionaries.

Farmer Participatory Approach

With accelerating global and greater awareness of the value of local knowledge, the need for good and timely information and insights become more clearly evident. There is, therefore, a need of more farmer's participatory approach for analysis of the situation, problem diagnosis, finding out alternative solutions, planning the course of action, monitoring, evaluation and feedback. The extension agent acts as a facilitator during the whole process and solutions to local problems are to be developed in partnership with farmers. Extension workers therefore need new skills such as rapport building, mobilizing and nurturing community organizations.

Farmer Demand-driven Extension

Under the T&V system the technology dissemination regime was more supply driven. Research and extension agendas were pre-set based on assumptions about issues in the rural areas. An important reason why research and extension were insensitive to farmers' problems was due to the lack of effective feedback system. The vast majority of small and marginal farmers, especially women, are not in a position to influence research and extension priorities. Therefore, what is required is a demand driven extension system that is driven by farmers' needs. For the purpose of improving the feedback systems, farmers need to be organized into functional groups such as Self Help Groups (SHGs). These groups can provide an effective channel for both the dissemination of technologies and they can provide an effective feedback to research and extension.

Privatization of Extension Services

The success achieved in agricultural development till date can be attributed largely to the efforts of the public sector extension. However, in the present era, with the growing importance to cutting-edge technologies it becomes difficult for the public sector extension to deliver the goods. Besides, the financial crunch is also adding to the pressure on the government to maintain the vast extension network. An effective alternative would be to delink certain services form the public sector and allow the private sector to handle those services. The draft policy framework for agricultural extension (2000- 2001) states that wherever possible subsidies will be phased out, in order to stimulate emergence of a private input supply network to provide hybrid seeds, artificial insemination services, fertilizers, biofertilizers, agro-chemicals, animal feed, machinery and equipment and other agricultural supplies and consultancy services to farmers on a full cost-recovery basis.

Cyber Extension

Access to information and improved communication is crucial requirement for agricultural development. However, it is observed that the rural population still has difficulty in accessing critical information in order to make timely decisions. Modern communication technologies when applied to rural areas can help improve communication, increase participation, disseminate information and share knowledge and skills. Cyber Extension would be the major form of technology dissemination in the near future. It uses the power of online networks, computer communications and digital interactive multimedia to facilitate dissemination of agricultural technology. The pilot projects of 'Warne Wired Village' in Kolhapur, Maharashtra and 'Information Villages' in Pondicherry have successfully demonstrated the acceptability and usage of Cyber Extension at village level.

Human Resource Development

A World Bank study of 192 countries reveals that only 16 per cent of growth is explained by physical capital (machinery, buildings and physical infrastructure), while 20 per cent comes from natural capital. But not less than 64 per cent can be attributed to human and social capital. There are about 1,00,000 public extension functionaries in the country. Keeping in mind the emerging trends in agricultural development, the extension workers will have to be adequately trained. A massive campaign is required for skill upgradation and capacity building of extension workers mainly on the subject matter areas of Participatory Rural Appraisal (PRA) techniques; community mobilization and organisation methods; development of leadership skills; management of common property resources; and conflict resolution between different interest groups.

Empowering Women

Women play a major role in farm activities but are less influential in the development process. Public extension system targeting women should take concerted efforts to promote women access to ownership of land; access to credit; to build technical competency on skill based technologies; to increase participation in decision-making.; to organise them into self help groups and; to develop their leadership abilities. The TANWA model, which is quite a success in Tamil Nadu, can be expanded further to cover all the villages.

Conclusion

In the process of modernization, the concerns such as ecology, globalization, rainfed agriculture, small farmers and agricultural labourers should be taken into account as they are vital to accomplish the goal of modernization i.e., sustainable agricultural development. The Extension system needs reorientation to meet the needs and requirements of the farmers. Knowledge revolution is currently taking place in all the business and industrial sectors.

Sound knowledge base in agricultural sciences is a key element to handle the agricultural education for the benefit of the farmers. If the income of the farmers increased per unit area by the intervention of new technologies or new varieties introduced by Extension workers, then the farmers will recognise the agricultural system. Technology transmission with commitment and involvement would always pay better. Official oriented extension would not survive in future but service oriented extension with commitment and challenge would be recognized by the farmers. A vibrant knowledge based, problem solving blended with sincere service minded extension worker can motivate and change the farmers for adoption of new varieties or new technologies.

I hope that the delegates of this Symposium will deliberate on such issues and come out with useful recommendations for Modernizing Indian Agriculture. I am happy to inaugurate the National Symposium on Modernizing Indian Agriculture in 21st Century – Challenges, Opportunities and Strategies.

REFERENCES

Bradford, K.J. and Cohn, M.A. 1998. Seed Biology and Technology at the Crossroads and Beyond. Introduction to the Symposium on "Seed Biology and Technology: Applications and Advances and Prospects for the Future". *Seed Science Research*. 8: 153-160.

Datt Ruddar and K.P.M. Sundharam.1998. *Indian Economy*. New Delhi: S. Chand and Company Ltd.

India 1996. A Reference Annual, Publications Division, Ministry of Information and Broadcasting, Government of India.

Jacob Viner. 1985. The Economics of Development. In: *Approaches to the Problem of Underdevelopment*. Ed: A.N.Agarwal and S.P.Singh, Oxford University Press. p.12.

James,C. 1998. *Global Status of Transgenic Crops*. APSA Publication.

Kannaiyan, S. 1999. Rural Agricultural Work Experience (RAWE) Programme for Under Graduate Agriculture Students. In *Experiential Learning System – Approach Rural Agricultural Work Experience* (ed.). S. Kannaiyan and R. Annamalai, Tamil Nadu Agricultural University, Coimbatore. pp.232-238.

Kannaiyan, S. 2000. *Hybrid Rice Research Status in the Philippines and China*

– *Visit Report*, Tamil Nadu Agricultural University, Coimbatore. pp.1-37.

Paroda, R.S. 1998. *Foreword in Accreditation for Quality Assurance in Agricultural Education*, ICAR, New Delhi.

Rao, M.V. 1997. Valedictory Address - Agricultural Development Perspective for the Ninth Five Year Plan: A Scientist's View Point. In: *Agricultural Development Paradigm for the Ninth Plan under New Economic Environment* (ed.) Desai. B.M., New Delhi: Oxford & IBH Publishing Co. Pvt. Ltd.

UNDP. 1996. *Human Development Report*. P.1.

3

MODERNIZING INDIAN AGRICULTURE IN 21st CENTURY TECHNOLOGY DEVELOPMENT

Some macro issues, opportunities and strategies for development

— *A. Venkataraman* and *Krishnaveni Muthiah*

The physical, social and economic environments of the world are changing fast. Technology is the prime driving force for these changes. The rate of change will accelerate steeply further in the 21st century. Explosion of knowledge in IT led communication sector, frontier areas of biotechnology – particularly in genetic engineering related to human medicine, and space exploration would open up vast opportunities for growth and promote change.

Technology driven growth in agriculture, comparatively, has slowed down in the dying decades of the 20th Century. The green revolution technology package has lost its steam. New dynamic breakthroughs in agricultural sciences and technologies are not in sight. Our rays of hope, for future spurt in growth, linger on anticipated contributions of biotechnology. So, far the present, efficient management of the existing systems and resources to meet the expanding market for agricultural produces appear to be the best option for promoting sustained growth.

This chapter reviews the emerging issues and opportunities facing the agricultural sector in the short run – a decade or two.

and suggests strategies for improving the effectiveness of the technology development system. It argues that a decentralized area specific integrated research establishment with developmental responsibilities, backed-up by a competent apex research framework at the State and national levels, is critical for development.

Environmental Changes, Emerging Issues and Opportunities

Demographic changes, economic growth, and social developments assisted by welfare measures of the State would, in the coming decades, exert strong and competing demands on the finite natural resources. Pressure on land-would increase sharply, squeezing land from agriculture and land based rural occupations. With improving standards of living, and urbanization and industrialization demand on water by various user groups would increase. Consequently availability of water for irrigation would decrease. Pollution of water resources, unless regulated effectively, would increase. Rational allocation of water and control of pollution would emerge as major areas of concern. Natural resource conservation and judicial use of the natural resources for maximum common good would progressively demand greater and greater public attention and care.

Over time, with economic growth, contribution of agriculture sector to the national GDP is steadily declining. This trend would continue. However agriculture, or land-based occupations, would continue to occupy a key position in the economic development agenda of the country. Agriculture sector would be the major livelihood provider for 60 to 65 per cent of the population, that too for the less endowed rural people. Besides, it would serve as the main plank for food and nutrition security of the nation and support agro based industries.

With growth in population and change in life styles demand for food is changing fast and this trend would accelerate. Supply of produces would need to match the expanding and changing demands in terms of both quantity and quality. Cost of produce would emerge as a major factor of concern; with WTO sponsored unrestricted market access unless Indian agriculture becomes competitive in quality and cost, imports would increase and export opportunities would disappear.

Since independence the national and State governments have been spearheading economic growth and social welfare through public policies and direct investments. The State is now involved in a wide array of assorted activities employing massive manpower. This is causing severe strain on the State finances. State intervention in developmental efforts on such a scale and range is neither needed nor sustainable any longer; even new assets created at great public cost are languishing for want of O&M. The need for redefining the State's role and confining it to select areas is receiving attention now.

With full-scale switch over to global market economy and further spurt in growth of IT industry the need for rationalizing the State's role would increase sharply. The State would have to shed off its direct involvement from certain spheres and facilitate local groups and private sector to play more active role in development. In future active association of people, including women, would be a key feature in development approach. Without public involvement sustainability of development as well as common assets would become the casualty.

Future Focus

It is vital to improve the performance of the agricultural sector significantly, and make it competitive to provide a stable base for the livelihood of the rural population and food and nutrition security for the nation. In an environment of shrinking natural resources, and emerging environmental concerns, growth in agriculture would have to come mainly through increased productivity. Technology, backed by effective public policies and efficient management of services would be the engine for growth.

Technology generation would continue to be the responsibility of the public sector, though funding would continue to be a limitation. This would necessitate judicious and productive use of the funds through proper planning and management. Private sector research efforts would be encouraged but it is likely to largely confine its attention to commercial areas with assured quick returns. So the effectiveness of public funded research would be a major factor of concern for development.

To infuse effectiveness in the public funded Technology Development system changes in public policies, institutional development and investment patterns are needed. Desirable changes in the system to face the emerging challenges follow.

Decentralize Research and Development

The country has a network of research stations supported by both the National and State governments. Research efforts of these institutions are coordinated through various institutional arrangements. The research system to be effective must have close linkage with the farmers and be alive to their local problems, limitations and opportunities. The country has been demarcated into a large number of agro climatic zones and decentralized zonal concept has been accepted as an effective service provider for development. To make it to happen Zonal Research Centres (ZRC) for perusing decentralized R&D have been established all over the country at great public cost as an integral part of the State Agricultural Universities. Despite heavy investments the concept has not yet been adequately institutionalized and made to function effectively. This weakness should be remedied.

ZRCs should be assigned primary responsibility for generating, scouting, screening, and integrating technologies for promoting sustained development of the agro climatic zone. It should act as the brain trust and prime mover for development. Its mandate must be redefined and its structure and functions must be recast.

The Zonal Centre must analyze developmental issues and opportunities from the angle of the people involved in farming and common societal needs, select technologies appropriate for sustainable development and promote developmental efforts. Agriculture development must be perceived in a broader framework and include natural resources conservation, and all land and water related pursuits by rural people.

The ZRC must survey the land and water resources of the zone and plan for optimum use of the natural resources. Soil fertility maintenance and management must receive great attention. Also, water conservation and use must receive equal attention. Pollution and environmental hazards must be controlled and if possible eliminated. The water balance of the zone must be reviewed and measures for effective use of irrigation resources and conservation of moisture of rainfed tracts must be designed and promoted. Efforts must be directed at using every single cent of land and each drop of water productively. Community assets must be preserved, developed and protected. The ZRC must develop, besides technology, public policies and suggest administrative measures for effectively ensuring natural resources conservation and development.

While designing research agenda focus must be on productivity enhancement, quality improvement and reduction of cost of production to make our produces competitive in the markets, both domestic and international. Research output must be environment friendly and must serve both irrigated and rainfed agriculture. Mixed farming as well as specialized farming, according to potentials and soundness of economics, must be promoted. Technology development and selection must address issues on land and water management, crop management, tree farming, and livestock including fisheries management. There is special need for selective mechanization of agriculture and promoting value addition at production centres.

Team effort would be required for making research cost effective. Duplicative research must be carefully avoided and research planning must receive great attention. With establishment of strengthened ZRCs smaller research stations within the zone can be, with advantage, phased out. Instead on-farm research involving progressive farmers must be promoted. Involving farmers at selection of suitable technologies will quicken adoption and dissemination process.

Social sciences must receive equal attention as biological

sciences. Social scientists must be involved in analyzing trends in agricultural production, natural resource use, market potentials, adoption patterns, and in suggesting corrective measures. Jointly with extension agencies the ZRC must research and suggest strategies for cost effective technology transfer and protection of common resources. Attaching the professional extension system to the ZRCs would be rewarding; it merits a review.

Skill development and enhancement are two prerequisites for sustained development and increased income generation. ZRCs must play a dominant role in Human Resource Development (HRD). Farmer education with responsibility for distance education must form yet another segment of responsibility of the ZRCs. Distance education and supportive institutional training courses must be varied in character and assist in technology transfer, entrepreneur development and skill development for a better livelihood.

There are goad potentials for export trade using tissue culture technologies; these must be exploited. As in the case of IT industries the nation has an advantage in productively using biotechnologies for producing seeds and seedlings and choice flowers for export. Though farmer training these technologies must be popularized by ZRCs.

Service facilities for testing soil, water, agricultural inputs, and processed products must be available at the ZRCs and operated on commercial lines. These facilities must be accessible to public and private sectors and individuals.

A senior and competent scientist, endowed with managerial abilities, must lead the ZRC. This person must have strong developmental orientation with empathy for farmers. The centre must have five units devoted to natural resources, production, protection, social sciences and education. The ZRC must have close liaison with district administration and must be managed by a board comprising scientists, farmer interests and development agencies. Public funds should support the institution based on a three-year plan, which must be reviewed and refined on an annual basis.

Supportive Framework

There must be a clear division of responsibilities between the ZRCs and the main campus of the State Agricultural Universities (SAU). The main campus, endowed with better resources, should focus on higher levels of researchable issues. It must formulate a proactive research plan on a relatively longer-timeframe, address macro issues relating to development and pick-up key thrust frontier areas like biotechnology, environmental sciences, crop-physiology, and other basic-research areas of concern for its direct attention. It should refine research processes and make them reliable and cost effective. Maintenance and introduction of genetic resources, export promotion, special area development, providing leadership in development of public policies on macro socio economic issues related to agricultural development and human resources development for higher responsibilities must also receive its attention.

All research activities needing controlled conditions and intensive laboratory support with sophisticated equipments must be undertaken in the main campus. This would assist prudent capital investments. The scientists of the main campus can work as partners in the zonal research programmes.

The SAUs must interact with the general universities of the State and benefit by the expertise available in biological sciences at these institutions. Besides, effective linkages with extension system and private industry, and national and international research systems must be continuously built up. The role of the main campus and teaching institutions of the SAUs would need to be refined and made cost effective with a view to enable their strategic role in research leadership and guidance effective. Such a refinement would, as a consequence, warrant structural changes at the national level as well. National research system should minimize its direct involvement in field research and focus on macro policy issues and direction setting and implementation guidance.

Vision

The reformed technology development system must aim at generating not less than a 4.5 per cent annual growth rate in agriculture. Ensuring food and nutrition security, reducing cost of production, conserving and improving natural resources, preventing pollution and thereby sustainable development must be its core objectives. In addition, assisting larger income generation in the rural sector and improving the quality of life of the society must be its driving force. Above all prosperity of humanity and not mere production enhancement should be the vision guiding technology development efforts.

4

INDIAN AGRICULTURE AT THE CROSS-ROADS AND THE STRATEGIES FOR TECHNOLOGY DEVELOPMENT AND TECHNOLOGY DISSEMINATION FOR MEETING THE CHALLENGES IN 21ST CENTURY

— *P.N Jha*

As rightly claimed, one of the most significant achievements that India could be proud of after getting freedom from British Rule, is the spectacular success achieved on food-front which is obvious from the fact that from a mere 50 million tonnes of foodgrains produced at the time of independence, we have produced 203 million tonnes of foodgrains in 1999-2000. In other words, there has been an increase in food production by four times. Despite this success and achieving of self sufficiency in food, there has not been stability as well as sustainability in the food production. Agriculture depends yet on nature to a great extent in many parts of the country. Because of recurring floods and droughts in one part of the country or the other, there is always a risk of being deficient in foodgrain despite the buffer stock that we have. This is mainly because of instability in foodgrain production as well as the galloping increase in population which has now crossed 100 crores. Therefore, to match the balance between increasing population and the increase in food production there is a need for stock taking of where we were, where we are and where we ought to go in so far as agricultural research and extension system are concerned.

It is estimated that by the year 2002, we shall require almost 230 million tonnes of foodgrains and by the year 2020, the requirement may go up to 300 million tonnes. While the area under foodgrain crops has been to the extent of around 123 million hectares and the average yield per hectare, in general, presently stands at 15.47 quintal. The coverage under irrigation is hardly 37 per cent. The percentage share of Agriculture in GDP is going down and presently it is 28 per cent.

Within the country, there is a wide variation from State to State, from region to region both in total production of foodgrains as well as in yield per hectare. For example, while in Punjab the average yield per hectare is about 36.84 quintals per hectare and in Haryana 27.30 per hectare, the same in Bihar is only 14.80 quintal per hectare and in Madhya Pradesh hardly 10.07 quintals per hectare. In Tamil Nadu, this figure comes to 21.02 which is the highest out of the Southern States but lower that what is in Punjab, Haryana and even in West Bengal. While the progress in Agriculture has been glaring but in yield per hectare, we are far behind many countries of the world. We may have quite higher ranks in matter of production, for example, in wheat, rice, sugarcane, groundnut, millets etc., but in yield per hectare, we are towards the bottom. The total production in different crops has increased mainly because we have a larger area under cultivation as compared to many other countries of the world.

Even today, India accounts for less than 1 per cent of agricultural exports including horticulture. This percentage has to be augmented to at least 3 per cent in the next few years, if agriculture has to become commercially and internationally viable and thus enabling us to compete in the global market. The value addition to the produce and to make the produce export worthy by maintaining the quality looking to the international consumer's choice and preferences, have to be one of the main planks of our agricultural strategy right in the beginning of the 2lst century.

First Generation Technology

The break-through in agricultural production was the result of green revolution on account of advent and popularization of high-yielding dwarf varieties of wheat and subsequently of some other crops like maize, sorghum, bajra (pearl millet) and rice. The first generation technology included high-yielding varieties including hybrids and composites, high doses of chemical fertilizers, emphasis on use of pesticides, fungicides, herbicides etc., intensive irrigation, multiple cropping and maximum tillage/tilth. All these led to an approach of capital-intensive agriculture. The result was immediate solving of the food problem and almost stoppage of imports from foreign countries. However, this positive up-stream gain and result of intensive agriculture and emphasis on use of chemicals were not free from mal-effects and there were so many down-stream consequences of this type of agriculture aimed at short-term gains rather than in long term perspective.

Down-stream Consequences of Higher Production/Intensive Agriculture

Deforestation, deterioration of soil health, increased soil salinity, the problem of water-logging, gradual depletion in ground water level and also pollution of ground water, environmental degradation, residual toxic effects of pesticides, destruction of many beneficial organisms and contamination of food chain were the glaring downstream consequences of intensive agriculture. Of course, the gap between rich and poor, have and have nots got widened and regional imbalances were sharper than ever before.

The Needed Shifts in Technology Development and the Strategy thereof

Most of the food production increased as a result of intensive agriculture in hardly 30 per cent of the cultivable/irrigated land while almost 70 per cent of the area in the country remains yet unexploited, rain-fed, mostly depending on nature full of problematic soils, wasteland, water logged, deep water area, visited by floods and simultaneously droughts as recurring features. Farmers of this vast area are also small and marginal farmers with a large percentage below the poverty line who can hardly afford costly inputs and capital investment. Therefore, in order to make farming sustainable and a business enterprise rather than being only risky and a way of subsistence living, a different approach both in the matter of technology development and also in technology dissemination will have to be devised and adopted.

The shifts in Technology Development may include economic yield maximization rather than simply yield maximization, holistic approach rather than the singular effort, marrying latest technology with ancient wisdom, investment in Human Resource Development, up-gradation of skills rather than more investment in materials and machineries, greater emphasis on organic/natural farming than on chemical farming, special research and extension efforts for exploiting the yield potential of rain-fed and dry land area and also of water logged, deep water and marshy land situations. Technology for reclaiming problematic soils like acidic and saline soils, shift to crops like pulses, oilseeds, cash crops like vegetables, fruits, medicinal and aromatic plants, tubers etc., are also called for. The overall approach has to be market-driven and demand-driven rather than being only supply and producer-driven. Much greater emphasis is needed on integration of plant-dairy-animal husbandry and the fisheries-poultry etc., and the overall farming system approach. Of course, the monsoon management and simulation models have also to be worked out for making the gray area green and for 'save green revolution' and to add strength, viability and to revive the fatigued green revolution. Systematic research and technology capsules for integrated nutrient management and integrated pest management have to receive priority attention.

Research thrusts have to be identified in the light of the priorities and the need of the hour as outlined above. Also, Research on Post Harvest Technology, Value Addition and Export Orientation, Research aimed at promoting equity rather than promoting disparity are also need of the time. Technology has to be so generated in order to suit the requirement of the small and marginal farmers as well as hilly and tribal regions. Instead of depending totally on Government and Public Sector machineries for research work, the time has come also for partly having Contract Services, Consultancy Services, Contract Research in an orchestrated synchronized manner.

There is a need for emphasis on research on Bio-Technology, Seed Technology, Bio-Chemistry, Micro-biology, Space Technology, Computer Technology, Information Technology, Agro Meteorology Technology, Dairy and Meat Technology, Market Technology, Educational Technology and Training and Extension Technology in order to give faster results as well as both short-term and long-term useful effects. The paradigm shift from green revolution to ever green revolution; from commodity centered approach to farming system approach have to be designed and put into operation both by the research and extension Agencies involved in the process. So far, the quality of food was never emphasized. It was only quantum of food that was the approach. However, with the nutritional deficiency looming large both in infants and adults irrespective of age, there is realization now that it is not only the quantity but also the quality of food that is no less important. Therefore, the approach has to be a policy for food-based diet rather than the drug-based approach. The food security and the nutritional security have to be major concerns.

Technology Dissemination and Extension Strategy

To revamp and accelerate sluggish agricultural growth, to preserve and improve the natural resources and bounties rather than allowing them to slip into degradation and bridging the regional disparities and reducing the widening gulf, an all-pronged strategy is needed. Looking to no less than 70 per cent of the rural population and 45 per cent of women population in the country, technological empowerment of rural populous particularly farm women and also adult farmers have to receive priority attention.

It is being gradually observed that there is a poor linkage and lack of coordination between the sister organizations working towards the same objectives. There is also, quite often, duplication of work and wastage of scarce public resources. There is hardly any mission mode approach. Improved methods of technology dissemination are seldom in large scale practice and the average farmer remains isolated from the main stream and there is less emphasis on human resource development. Therefore, new initiatives are called for to remove these shortcomings. There has to be a strong linkage between the ICAR Institutes, State Agricultural Universities, KVKs., other Government and non-Govt. organizations working in the area as well as the Rural Organizations in order to pool in the resources and work in a harmonious manner to bring faster result and to avoid duplication of efforts. This will also save a lot of men and material resources.

The ICAR has rightly initiated the Technology Transfer system passing through the stages of Technology Assessment, Technology Refinement and Technology Integration through IVLP and KVKs. Analysis of cost-risk return structure of major farming systems in different agro-eco regions is called for. There has to be a consensus on the unifying and well-tested recommendations to the farmers in order to avoid conflicting recommendations passing through the pipeline. Instead of depending on one method of communication or one extension method, it is always better to advocate and use a multiple combination of methods and media mix to have a well-pronounced effect on the mind of the farmers. The time has come for rationalization and consolidation of KVKs and Farmers' Training Centres. There has to be a formal institutional linkages and feedback mechanism from fields/farmers to pass on the feedback to the research system for improvement in technology. This will help in identifying the hidden bugs in the technology and help the scientists in drawing technical programme for bringing refinement and improvement in the technology generated by them. This has to be in a cyclic process i.e., scientists to farmers and farmers to scientists, the extension agents in between the two playing the role of catalysts and helping both ends to benefit from each other. Apart from institutional training of farmers, farm women and farm youth at KVKs and at Research Stations of the ICAR and SAUs, emphasis is to be laid on peripatetic/mobile training so that the scientists go to the fields and farmers are trained right in the fields in the villages. Moreover, it will give an idea to the KVK. scientists about the first hand reaction of the farmers and as to how the technology disseminated is doing at the grass-root level. The recent bio-village concept as emphasized by no less a person than Dr. M.S. Swaminathan could be tried in other parts of the country as well. This concept is said to be the path-way for rural prosperity which can generate job-led growth, not job-less growth. As emphasized earlier in the beginning of the Community Development Programme, when Information Centres were established in villages particularly at Block/Taluka level, there have to be an added stress on Information and Technology shops in villages and Agril. Technology Information Centres at the main and the Regional Research and Extension Stations/Centres.

The cherished goal of the next 47 years i.e., the time by which India reaches the stage of Centenary Celebration of her independence should be to wipe out the tears from everyone's eyes, remove the gap between rich and poor, provide full food and nutritional security to the populace and ensure women empowerment and emancipation. All these can be achieved by making agriculture fully sustainable, raising the share of agricultural exports in work market and eradicating poverty in all its manifestations. It is, therefore, rightly thought that Indian agriculture is now at its cross-roads and in order to develop agriculture in all its ramifications, sustained and multi prompt strategies have to be adopted, many of which have been elaborated in the preceding paragraphs.

These cherished goals in the 2lst century when achieved will go a long way in realizing the dream of Mahatma Gandhi, the Father of the Nation, for whom the political freedom of 1947 was only half of the race won while the rest half was to come from economic emancipation and freedom.

5

MODERNIZING INDIAN AGRICULTURE IN 21st CENTURY

Challenges, Opportunities and Strategies

— M. Swamiappan

With an everlasting increase in Indian population, there is an emergent need to augment food production on a continuous basis. The present production of 206 million tonnes of foodgrains production can be increased to 440 million tonnes even with the available farm resources if put to effective use. Retrospection of agricultural development in India, that took place in the last century, instils confidence on the stakeholders to face the challenges that are predicted by the changing socio-economic scenario of the millennium 2000. It has been clearly demonstrated beyond doubt, that the investment in agricultural research and development could bear fruit with multiple effects. The country has been turned into the state of surplus from that of deficit, particularly in foodgrains. People have started consuming not only more food, but also quality food. Supply of raw materials to agro-based industries has started increasing substantially. Agri-export basket has started bulging with varied assortments, netting sizable foreign exchange. Thus, the country has now smoothly stepped into the new millennium 2000. However, there is no room to feel complacent with what we have achieved so far in the field of agricultural development.

Challenges Ahead

The Rio conference made each and every country in the globe to become aware of the urgency of sustaining the ecological environment and the habitat of human beings. The emergence of WTO has changed the dimension and magnitude of challenges in the global market. Revolution in *Information Technology* has narrowed down the time involved in the diffusion of agricultural technologies. Biotechnology is currently emerging as yet another scientific base to revolutionalize Indian agriculture. The political scenario particularly in many developing countries is not going to be as stable as it was, however, the liberalized economic approach in our nation is going to be the centre-piece of our planned development. The Indian population has touched almost one billion mark and it is expected to grow at the rate of 1.2 per cent per annum in the near future. Still, 30 per cent of our population lives in absolute poverty. Thus, the global agro and socio economic scenario is predicted to be turbulent and challenging. How are we to face these challenges and alleviate poverty through agricultural development? The answer is not a near sight but our strategic planning and implementation would certainly pave way for our success in Agricultural and Agro-Industry Development.

The rapid change in agriculture has also brought forth new areas for concern. In the beginning, the sole aim of the agricultural scientists was to increase the food production. Today we have moved from food production to the problems of equity, environmental sustainability and export agriculture. To tackle these new challenges the horizons of agricultural sciences have also developed new concepts and methodologies.

Future Strategies

It is an indisputable fact that, it is only through the advancements of science and technology and their applications at faster rate in agriculture could help the human race to face the challenges in pushing up the frontiers of production, mitigating the socio-economic problems and in alleviating poverty.

A high growth rate of agriculture has become essential to remove poverty and unemployment and to ensure food as well as nutritional security. All calculations indicate that a 50 per cent of the increase in employment opportunities have to come from agriculture. If the economy is to grow at seven per cent per annum and if the export base were to expand, the value of agricultural output must increase at an annual rate of 4.5 per cent between 2000 and 2005. Particularly, a very substantial increase in growth rate is required in the case of pulses, oilseeds, fruits and vegetables. In order to achieve rapid diversification in agricultural sector, the growth in avenues such as dryland horticulture, commercial floriculture, medicinal and aromatic plants must be accelerated. At the same time, without sacrificing the need for self-sufficiency in food, efforts should be directed to bring about changes in cropping mix to enable the farmers to earn higher income.

It is, therefore, important that future managers of agricultural development must have a better understanding of globalization issues as in relation to the Indian agri-business sector. A meaningful strategy is needed to sustain the food production. The efforts need to be harnessed in an integrated fashion encompassing all the partners responsible in the agricultural sector.

New Avenues of Investment

The new avenues of investments which the economic liberalization has opened up are: commercial horticulture, floriculture, aquaculture, tree growing, mushroom production, processing of sugar, fibre and oilseed crops and exportable grains. In horticulture, mango, grapes, banana and select vegetables provide ample scope for export market. More is talked about export of cut flower and orchids. An All India Policy Draft is being ready to promote medicinal plants and patenting the medicines from these plants. Near revolution is taking place in "prawn farming" in the inland and coastal belts while corporate companies are launching large scale production of mushroom production for exports. Hundreds of small business have entered in mushroom production, of course, mostly concentrated in cities and towns. Expansion in sugar production capacity is the order of the day in many States. New oilseed crops such as soyabean and sunflower are grown in larger areas than before. Dairy sector thus far has been the monopoly of cooperatives and recently corporate firms are making entry into this area.

Technology, Agro-Processing and Export

As in the other sectors of Indian economy, agricultural sector is increasingly integrated with global market. The high quality demand of international market has made more and more-agro-processing and input firms to stay "Hi-tech". Currently, technology tie-up with foreign firms is becoming more common, an essential pre-requisite to sell our products in the global market. Such kind of technology import is resorted for production of milk produces, egg products, herbal extraction, prawn farming, cut flowers, tissue culture plants, hybrid seed production, bio-pesticides, pressure irrigation systems, milling of scented varieties of rice, fruit and vegetable processing and packing, etc. This trend expedites modernization of agro-processing in India. This is critical to achieve export targets.

Economic liberalization has unambiguously demonstrated its influence on export of non-conventional export items. Between 1992-93 and 1995-96, the export value of fruits and vegetables claimed up from about Rs. 800 crore to Rs. 1290 crore. Flowers and seeds have risen from Rs. 17 to 60 crore.

Looking Ahead

The economic reforms pursued in the past few years has started to give a clear and positive impact on agriculture. It has injected a new dynamism in the agricultural and associated activities. WTO has opened up new opportunities for India's agricultural products, both fresh and processed. Investment on value addition to agricultural products may generate significant income and environment and enlarge the scope for export of farm products. The expanding capital market in India has been central to the investment on agro-processing and the commercialization of agriculture and capital market need better nurturing.

It is important to ensure more favourable policy environment such that capital formation in agriculture is accelerated. In fact, gross capital formation in agriculture between 1985-1986 and 1995-1996 is poor. Decentralized production of agricultural commodities tied with large processing, marketing and export firms, must be encouraged so as to ensure equity with development while major thrust may be market driven development of agricultural and other sectors in the Indian economy. It is critical that special sectors such as health, education, social infrastructure and food security must receive adequate attention till such time we could make a dent on poverty.

Historical experience shows that adequate infrastructure is a pre-condition for economic development. Larger investment on infrastructure such as roads, storage and marketing, telecommunications, shipping yards and air strips, power, etc. are important to ensure sustained growth in agriculture and other sectors. It is a universal fact that a growing economy will cause negative externalities on environment. There must be a system of both control and concessions to encourage environmental protection. Finally, there may be market failures in some cases and in some occasions, when the economy is integrated with rest of the world. There may not be a level playing field for domestic producers. In these situations government must intervene to ensure viability of the economic activities. It must be more so in the case of agriculture. Last but not the least is adequate measures to be taken up to boost R&D in important areas like crop diversification, livestock farming, horticulture and biotechnology.

Conclusion

I am happy to note that the issues facing the country in the 21st century have been discussed under four major themes, namely, Technology Development, Technology Dissemination, Technology Utilization and Policy Issues.

This is a unique Symposium organized under the auspices of the International Extension Forum, Society of Extension Education and the Tamil Nadu Agricultural University. Totally 70 participants from Kerala, A.P., M.P., Punjab, Delhi and Karnataka States have participated in the deliberation and papers have been presented and discussed in detail.

The recommendations that have emerged are noteworthy and need due attention by the authorities. Implementation of these recommendations will go a long way in making suitable improvements in all the sectors.

There is hardly any doubt to say that Agriculture will continue to be the backbone of India. The Tamil Nadu Agricultural University feels it a privilege to have hosted this National Symposium and I am happy for having delivered the valedictory address and distributed the certificates to the delegates, best paper presenters and Members of the Organizing Committee.

6

MODERNISING INDIAN AGRICULTURE IN 21st CENTURY

Challenges, Opportunities and Strategies

— *G. Perumal*

Modernising Indian Agriculture – What to Modernise? How modernising is going to improve the qualitative aspect of Indian Agriculture? Is it a new terminology that we are trying to understand in this century. Which sectors (Research, Technology transfer and technology users) are lacking modernising or all the three needs modernising. Do we have any measuring techniques to identify the needed areas to be modernized? Are we not trying and using for the past several decades the modern techniques and improved the qualitative and quantitative aspects of Indian Agriculture? Therefore, the word modernising, needs a new dimension and new definitions to implement the new programmes. Accordingly, our present thinking of the 21st century modernising should be different from the past century. Modernising normally means is a change process through which alteration occurs in the structural and functional units of the social system. Therefore, while attempting to change the process, consideration should be given to link the traditional and indigenous knowledge system for sustainable long lasting development. This is because, the indigenous and traditional knowledges were evolved from our environment. In other words, you are not an organism in an environment but you are environorganism.

Further, modernising means different things to different people at different places. Today's modernising may not fit in to tomorrow's society if we alter the system ignoring the environs of the social system. The agricultural sectors are composed of several parts and several actors. Hence, modernising Indian Agriculture should be viewed holistically. This means all the sectors/components such as teaching of future agriculture and its vision, the agricultural research and its changing roles, the transfer of technology and its different dimensions, the user systems and its capacity for the total involvement, the natural resources which influences modernising should be taken into consideration. Therefore, we have to think, perceive and act using our past experiences because past gives birth to present and the present strengthens our belief for tomorrow.

According to my personal views, modernising is not the computer knowledge of the researcher/extension agents or the possession of number of software equipments, and the creation of sophisticated infrastructural facilities in an institution. But, modernising will be successful only when the scientists, extension functionaries, supporting agencies and the farmers totally involve in their respective fields in a coordinated manner, by availing the applied knowledge with competence besides delivering the appropriate timely services.

Of late, there are several agencies such as the input agencies, private agencies, NGOs, mass media, research institutions, co-operatives, financial institutions and farmers associations that are involved besides public sector extension in the development of agriculture and allied enterprises. If we carefully examine the changing nature of Indian Agriculture it will be clear that how much damage we have made in the past not only in the natural resource management but also the behaviour of scientists, extension functionaries and also the farmers only to meet the food requirements of the country, ignoring the allied enterprises for all-round development of agriculture. Though we have achieved self sufficiency in food production we have lost many things by performing self styled organisations forgetting to look into the problems in a holistic views. In other words, each one of us were working in isolation with ego. Now the time has come to plan our future systematically and usefully giving real meaning to 'Modernising Indian Agriculture'. Therefore, it is suggested that the following are the changing trend of Indian Agriculture and require special attention when we think of real modernising the agriculture. We have to plan accordingly to change the agriculture situation in the country using our past experiences for the betterment of the future in the context of problems, perspectives and also developing suitable strategies. Some are listed here:

- *Stagnating productivity :* The productivity of major crops has shown stagnation and in some cases even less than the normal yields – where we went wrong?
- *Subsistence remain the same :* Modernising here requires superior performance in research management, both in rainfed and irrigated agriculture. Do we have a new strategy?
- *Striking reduction in resource base :* This is due to inappropriate and unscientific use of natural resources including land and water. What the new natural resource management strategy?
- *Changes observed in food habits :* According to a survey, per capita cereal consumption of food declined observably, while the consumption of fruits, vegetables., dairy products showed increasing trend. The increased demand needs modern application of action knowledge by the farmers. What new dimensions we are going to propose?
- *Changing Farming Situations (Farm Diversification) :* It is observed that the area under foodgrain production is showing a declining trend. While there is an increasing trend is noticed in the case of non-food crops. This needs our special attention.
- *Rainfed Agriculture as neglected area :* Modernising rainfed agriculture is observed as a potential area for future agricultural growth. This has to be achieved by converting the knowledge based technology into situational based technology keeping in mind the potential resource constraints involving total community action. How to implement?
- *Private Extension :* Whether we recommend or not, the private extension is going to emerge as major extension

providers. When such is the case in what capacity, the public sector organisations can perform effectively and efficiently in a pluralistic institutional environment. How to make use of the private capabilities in the future Modernisation process.

- *Organisational Policy* : From 1960s to till date, several Agricultural Universities are emerging with prototype model. The ICAR institutes are also functioning more or less in the similar pattern. Do we need such parallel organisations? Then, what will be the Government policy to bring these two under one umbrella and function as *Single Window System*, so that the rare available resources can be used economically and efficiently in coordinated manner. Can we suggest new policy?
- *Accountability:* It is a fact that work culture both in SAUs; Government Departments and also in ICAR institutes, in short in all the public funded institutions are fading. In such situations, how to develop work efficiency/accontability among scientists, extension functionaries and with what policy framework. If the human power fails, then what to modernise?
- *Support Services* : We have failed in our efforts so far in improving services to all the categories of farmers through public machineries. So, in the present day circumstances how to make use of the efforts of public agencies, private sector and farmers groups/associations for providing the modern extension services to different strata of the farming community including women and youth. Do we have modern support service systems?
- *Zero Growth Technology* : It is an overall observation of the general public that no major breakthrough in the technology development emerged from the research systems. Further, the available technologies are also not able to influence the farming community. How to improve the existing system to meet the future challenges?
- *Changing Rural Scene* : Urban impact on rural people is gradually invading. Their contact with outside world and their information seeking behaviour is changing day by day. How to make use of this change for the advantages of modernising agriculture?

- *What Reform Model can Help Modernising :* Recent thinking towards diversification, commercialization, sustainability, accountability and emphasis on efficiency needs a new type of reforming to support modernising efforts. Several SAUs and SDAs are experimenting changes in their approaches all over the country. To overcome these problems can we think of creating an Agricultural Development Corporation (ADC) by integrating all the agricultural developing sectors including the State Agricultural Universities under one umbrella and one unified organisation. To what policy framework this can be effected?
- *Agricultural Education :* Modernizing Agricultural Education means revamping the method of teaching learning process with vision, training and implementation. Can we think of new modification in the curricula and syllabi considering the following few areas:

– Developing competency to take up agri-clinics (Capacity building).
– Re-modifying the RAWE programme.
– Imparting first hand knowledge about agro-based/Commercial agri firms/Post harvest Technologies.
– Knowledge and understanding of markets and its influence on Agri-business.
– Developing competency to handle different enterprises Agri/ Horti/Animal Husbandry etc. (functional knowledge).
– Help the students to help themselves in their own careers.

Prevent post-harvest losses : We have made very few efforts in preventing and modernising post-harvest losses. All the crops such as cereal, oilseeds, pulses, horticultural crops and also animal products needs modernising in productivity, value addition and also suitable export policy. Can we develop a suitable strategy now?

Avail elders expertise : Experienced retired scientists' services are available at the doorsteps of all the universities in the country. Involve and share their knowledge and expertise through organised seminars, workshops and discussions for the benefit of young scientists.

Finally, I want to bring the following ill planned programmes without Government's strong policy and commitments. We have learned lot of lessons from these projects and programmes.

1. Rice cultivation in Punjab,
2. Oil Palm,
3. Sericulture,
4. Cultivation of Tea in Nilgiris,
5. Inland Fish culture, and
6. Sugarcane cultivation, etc.

For want of time, I am unable to explain the various problems encountered in the implementation of these projects.

Finally, I request all the participants to involve in the two days deliberation and contribute your might to build up new strategies for modernizing the Indian Agriculture in the real sense in coming years.

SECTION II : TECHNOLOGY DEVELOPMENT

7

PARTICIPATORY TECHNOLOGY DEVELOPMENT

The Need of the New Millennium

— *Rajula Chandran*

Emphasis on a systems perspective in agricultural research requires a complete reversal of the technology generation approach viz., a farmer first or farmer participation approach where farmers are fully involved at all stages of technology development. The accomplishment of increasing food production and improved human welfare warrants a strong participatory client-centred research programme. Participatory research is a systematic process involving people in the analysis of their own situations. Farmer participatory research is a term increasingly used in agricultural research and development circles. It is a subject that is increasingly making people sit and think. At the least it underpins a refreshing new approach to indigenous environmental knowledge that goes further than just passive admiration. At the most it is a potentially important new direction for research and extension. In the context of shrinking resource base, agriculture in future can be sustained only by producing more food, fuelwood, fibre and other commodities from less land, less water and less energy per unit of output without the accompaniment of ecological harm. The stress on 'farmer participation' has arisen from a realization that earlier approaches to on-farm research recognized the importance of farmers, but was not able to effectively incorporate farmers' skills and experimental practices into the research process.

Definition

To define participatory technology development, it is a systematic process, which involves people in the analysis of their own situation. It gives them the skills and confidence to understand their own situations. (Tandon *et al.*, 1984)

It is research structured by the democratic interaction of the researcher and oppressed classes of people, and takes the form of a dialectical unification of theory and practice reciprocally between the researcher and the oppressed classes.

Concept of Participatory Technology Development

Participatory technology development is a three-pronged activity: a method of social investigation involving the full participation of the community; an educational process; and a means of taking action for development.

In its ideal form it involves the community actively in the research process and the subject of the research originates, is analyzed and solved by the community.

Learning about the indigenous technology and process through which such technologies were developed or innovated is very important because such innovations are made within the whole farming system under which the farmers operate and they show that resource poor farmers manage to modify and exploit micro-environments and climates (Jiggins, 1986).

Evolution of Participatory Technology Development

A quiet methodological revolution has occurred through three intermingling streams of innovation: Rapid Rural Appraisal (RRA) originating in the late 1970s; Rapid Assessment Procedures (RAP) developed in the 1980s with anthropological approaches and most recently, Participatory Rural Appraisal, a versatile semi-structured process of learning from, with and by rural people about rural conditions. In Rapid Rural Appraisal, much of the mainstream has been concerned with farming systems and livelihood. Participatory Rural Appraisal evolved as an outgrowth of Rapid Rural Appraisal. Advantage of PRA is its ability to generate in short time, information that can be used by development planners. The three, though their emphasis differ, all these approaches share an underlying rigour in the application of principles.

Need for Participatory Technology Development (PTD)

It is now widely accepted that small-scale farmers often have within their social, economical and environmental circumstance, technologies, which it would be wise to preserve. It is also realized that the scientific and development community has much to learn from what farmers do. In turn the 'scientific community' has some things to offer. These offerings could be categorized as facilitation of scientific and economic analysis of what farmers do, supporting adaptations of techniques to achieve greater, easier or more economic production and facilitation of access to technologies or resources which may alleviate constraints to adoption of local or improved practices. There is therefore, an explicit link between 'evaluation' or the analysis of performance of local practices, 'development' or supporting their performance and 'dissemination' or relieving the constraints to adoption. All these call for activities and methods to encourage participation of men and women farmers in developing agricultural technologies: this is the essence of Participatory Technology Development (PTD).

Steps in Participatory Technology Development

1. *Getting started*

The way the participatory research workers from outside a community choose an area to work in, introduce themselves and negotiate with the community about how they are going to work together, depends in its details on the context. This involves building up a relationship of confidence aimed at cooperation with farmers and making a joint analysis of the existing situation, farming systems and problems.

Village appraisal can be done effectively by using the PRA/RRA techniques. The major ones are :

(i) *Participatory mapping :* In participatory mapping and modelling, the villagers prepare maps or models of the village profile with chalks, colours and other material either on ground or on paper. Such maps may be of dwelling in the village, of farms and fields, water collections, forests, soils etc.

(ii) *Participatory transects :* It involves systematic walking with the villagers through an area discussing about the aspects of village life observed during the walk. It may relate to people, resources, soil, technology etc.

(iii) *Time line :* In this technique, a historical account is given by the villager of how different aspects of village life have changed. Since it is difficult to remember exact dates, the villager may be helped to broadly connect the changes with major events, political regimes or a cluster of year

2. *Looking for Things to Try*

The process of looking for things to try includes:

- determining the range of topics of concern and curiosity,
- screening indigenous technical knowledge and past experimentation –gathering promising ideas from outside the villages,
- research agreement on the research agenda.

Techniques to gather indigenous technical knowledge on specific topics are :

(i) *Making diagrams :* This is simply the visual presentation of data and causal relationships. Diagrams include representations of space, such as sketch maps of landuse around a village or homestead and transects; representation of time such as cropping and other seasonal calendars.

(ii) *Case Histories :* Farmers describe what was the original problem, what alternative ideas were considered and where these originated, what steps the farmer took to try out each of these ideas and why they chose that way, what failed and what worked well and why?

(iii) *Critical incident :* The aim here is to focus discussion on a key event in the recent past, in order to explain changes that have occurred, such as in environmental management or crop husbandry.

(iv) *Inventory of Farmers' Indicators :* Collecting the local terminology and indicators used in a certain technical field and trying to detect the meaning underlying these terms.

3. *Designing Experiments*

Aim of this activity is to develop experimental designs that suit the farmers' purposes and enrich their capacity. Three kinds of farmer experiments are defined.

(i) *Curiosity experiments :* Farmers set-up such experiments just to test an idea that comes to mind. It may or may not have an immediate practical end, but is stimulated fundamentally by curiosity.

(ii) *Problem-solving experiments :* Farmers' are keen to seek solutions to old and new problems through experimentation. Propensity to experiment and try out new ideas may be more pronounced in areas of diversified agriculture and poor extension services than in developed countries with less diversification and excellent research and extension facilities.

(iii) *Adaptation experiments :* These are conducted by farmers after they acquire a new technology or observe a demonstration technology promoted by an extension agency.

4. *Trying Out*

This includes not only actually doing the experiments and related activities, such as measurement and evaluation but also development of the capacity to implement and monitor experiments. The expected outcome is a growing number of experiments, with technologies of increasing complexity, are implemented and evaluated systematically.

5. *Sharing Results with Others*

This involves communication of results with other local and scientific methods to scrutinize and interpret them, and to encourage others to adapt and test the results for their circumstances.

Outcome of this activity is enhanced farmer to farmer diffusion of ideas and technologies, an increasing number of villages involve themselves in processes of organized technology development, making use of experiences of other communities and a farmer managed system of inter-village training and communication.

6. *Sustaining and Consolidating the Process*

Participatory research teams have to be concerned with organizational development and the creation of other favourable conditions for ongoing experimentation and development of sustainable agro-ecological systems. This involves assisting participatory research groups to consolidate, strengthening consolidation of inter-village cooperation by stimulating linking up with existing or developing new farmers organization at area level and developing locally manageable systems for monitoring the experimentation and diffusion process and its impact on the agroecological system and the livelihood of the communities involved.

The above linear steps may not always occur instead there are iterations, gaps and overlaps.

How to Increase the Amount of Participation?

(i) *Create enthusiasm :* The amount of constructive participation in a programme depends on the amount of enthusiasm it can generate. Programme salaries can be given but they should never overshadow enthusiasm as the principle driving force behind the programme.

(ii) *Start the programmes small and simple :* Many programmes are so large and complex that meaningful participation by the villagers is impossible. Once this error is committed, programme invariably takes one of two courses of action, either outsiders run the programme in perpetuity or the programme is turned over to villagers before they are at all capable of running it.

(iii) *Be careful with the role of outsiders :* Outsiders, both national and expatriates should be chosen for their willingness to live close to the people and their ability to establish friendships of mutual trust and candid two way communication.

(iv) *Plan for the phase-out of outsiders and of the programme itself :* One over-present goal of all programmes should be the eventual takeover by small farmer management. Thus, from the beginning, every activity should be organized in such a way that villagers will learn how to manage it and, if necessary, how to sustain it once the programme closes down.

(v) *Teach farmers to conduct small scale trials :* Only when small farmers know how to experiment with new technology will they achieve maximum possible independence of outside sources of information and be able to participate in the development of the steadily changing technology required by a productive agriculture.

(vi) *Don't try to meet all of the people's needs :* Programmes normally have to expend a good deal of effort to motivate people to try out recommended innovations. The inefficiency caused by trying to do everything at once, so widely observed among the better-motivated programme, becomes almost inevitable.

Points for Success in Participatory Technology Development

The success of participatory technology development depends on–

(i) *Researcher*

The researcher should possess:

(a) Basic respect for rural people,
(b) Interest in what they know, say and show;
(c) High levels of creativity and flexibility, and
(d) Humility.

Researcher must be:

(e) Willing to look at new problems and be able to adopt research methods to the farmers production system,
(f) A part of an inter-disciplinary team and be capable of contributing to the evaluation of dynamic social process, and
(g) Willing to take part in a mutual learning process with the community as well as to contribute specialized information in down-to-earth language which will stimulate the process itself.

(ii) *Research*

(a) Activities should be carried out on a community basis and with individual farmers only upon community approval.
(b) Research conducted in a community should be planned so that it is action oriented and it directly benefits that community.
(c) Setting the research agenda as a joint effort of community farmers and project researcher.
(d) Involve farmers in all phases of the research process including problem definition, trial design and implementation, recording

and analysis of results and readjustments for future research.

(e) Participatory village research should also have to incorporate the government officers and political leaders on all the levels in the common inquiry which then become a form of self-elimination for those who are charged with the responsibility over the different aspects of development.

Research Plan

(a) Development research requires an inter-disciplinary team approach. This in turn would lead to research planning in large units rather than in isolated piecemeal projects.

(b) Research involving people is by its very nature an educative process for all the categories of people involved in the process. This aspect should be given recognition in research planning.

(c) In the selection of problems to be tackled it must be kept in mind that it is easier to work in areas where the technological weight of the constraint is greater than the social one.

(d) Large measures of institutional flexibility especially at the field level are required.

(e) Research plan must be simple and specific enough to permit their rapid modification or adjustment to new findings.

Research Result

Participatory technology development is often seen to have more of a flavour of extension than of research. When farmers are involved in the research process, there is a need to orient it towards action. The difference between extension and participatory research is that. in participatory research, the aims are to identify problems and to test and evaluate possible alternatives together with farmers.

The most appropriate kind of initial research for communities where the original structure is weak is technology validation. In cases where adaptive research is necessary from the beginning this stage can be carried out with individual farmers with the approval of the community. The group must become incorporated into this process as soon as possible, or there will be a tendency for the individual participants to gain an advantage over the group as a whole, resulting in further social and economic differentiation.

Participatory Technology Development – Strengths

(i) Indigenous technology is respected and promoted
(ii) Encourages farmers to be innovative
(iii) It incorporates farmers' wishes
(iv) Makes use of cheap and locally available material
(v) It can empower individual farmer and rural communities
(vi) Strengthens link between farmer, extension worker and researcher
(vii) Farmer experimentation directs the research agenda
(viii) PTD ensures sustainability of technology
(ix) It involves farmers in all stages of technology development

Participatory Technology Development – Weaknesses

(i) It takes more time and resources initially
(ii) The site specificity limits the spread of technology
(iii) PTD requires a culture of openness and sharing – some village culture hinders the PTD process
(iv) It requires skills. change of attitude and flexibility of mind on the part of both farmers, extension and research staff, which is often lacking
(v) Unsystematic experimentation may lead to false conclusions

Conclusion

A systematic programme focused on the role of local innovation, ingenuity and intuition is undoubtedly an exciting new direction in terms of resource conservation. It comprises joint action, and disdains the temptation to sit back and admire local ingenuity. Participatory technology development is most commonly described as an integral activity that combines social investigation, educational work and action. In participatory research emphasis is on farmers' knowledge and research is then based on this. While necessity may indeed be 'the mother of invention, that proverb would be too simplistic an explanation, and would ignore the inherent creativity of many innovators. As our aim is now to use low cost and no cost technology, participatory research can be very well used to cull out such practices seen among farmers. Also due to the use of chemicals and fertilizers pollution and health hazards have become common now-a-days. A deep look into the farmers' living conditions has revealed that they have good natural management practices. So all these can be extracted and popularized to other places.

In such a way, participatory technology development is emerging as an alternative in agricultural research and can help to go a long way through

REFERENCES

Jiggins, J. 1986. Eastern, Central and Southern Africa. New directions. RRDC Bulletin Sutherland, A. Martin and Salmon, J .1998. 'Recent experiences with participatory technology development in Africa: Practitioners' Review.' *ODI Natural Resource Perspectives* #25. London.

Tandon, R..L.Vijay, Gothoskar and Orlando Lugo. 1984. *How to conduct Participatory Research among Women.* Society for Participatory Research in Asia . New Delhi.

8

TECHNOLOGY DEVELOPMENT AS A STRATEGY FOR MODERNIZING INDIAN AGRICULTURE DURING THE NEW MILLENNIUM

— B.K. Narayana Swamy

Many times several past investigations have only indicated whether the recommended technologies have been adopted or not by farmers. This gives percentage of farmers adopted the technology, but not the percentage of technologies adopted by the farmers. No doubt agricultural research in India has contributed new varieties of crops and new production technologies and increased production. However, many technologies available are not appropriate for diffusion. Encyclopedia of science and technology says systematic knowledge and action applicable to any recurrent activity is a technology. This has no exception to agricultural technologies. However, agricultural technologies involves the application of science and knowledge for practical use of technologies among farmers. Further, technology is any technique or method or equipment or product or process used as a tool in the context of agriculture i.e., all farm inputs, practices processes and services designed to reduce the uncertainty in achieving the desired target. Most of the technologies generated in India are not appropriate as revealed by large number of research and evaluation studies conducted in the country. Further, the system dealing with production technologies for farmers in the country failed to meet the fundamental needs of farmers because of its inappropriateness and least functioning efficiency. During the new millennium to meet the demands of growing population. However, several technologies developed through research were not tested under real farming conditions in the country. Further, farmers and extension workers were not involved in technology generation process resulted in inappropriateness of technologies. Thus, there is an urgent need for a model to develop appropriate technologies to modernize Indian agriculture. This technology development process should cover all the requirements with proper decisions at all stages of activities. The model should consider all the minute details needed for technology development. Further, the technology should have certain attributes for its wider adoption. Attribute regarded as the effect of a stated cause. Even though several technologies are identified in agriculture but the factors that influence the rate of diffusion of a technology can be viewed from different angles. However, Narayana's Lotus Model explains appropriate technology should have four major attributes with seven sub-items under each head for modernizing Indian agriculture like Relative advantage (Market feasibility, Market stability, Cost, Net profit, Profit consistency, Utility potential and Time saving), Compatibility (Cultural, Social, Physical, Psychological, Situational Relational and Anticipated), Practicability (Point of origin, Access to advice, Visibility, Mastery, Trialability, Demonstrability and Communicability), Complexity (Failure probability; Discomfort saving, Resource complexity, Reversibility, Work efficiency, Cognitive complexity) and Need Application complexity and need for development of more viable appropriate technologies.

The professional involved in technology development should consider four major attributes for technology development to modernize Indian agriculture as shown in Narayana's Lotus Model Fig. 8.1. The four attributes of appropriate technology are explained below.

Narayana's Lotus Model to Develop Appropriate Technologies for Modernizing Indian Agriculture

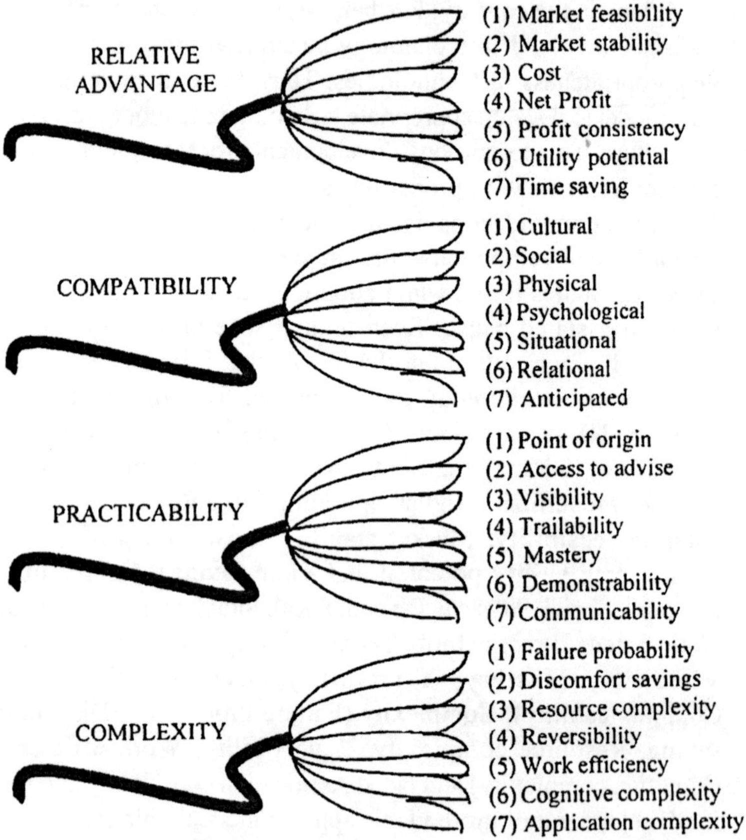

Fig 8.1 : Four attributes with sub-components are shown on the lotus for appropriate technology.

A. Relative Advantage

Relative advantage is the degree to which an innovation is superior to the idea it supercedes. The Relative advantage of an innovation can be explained with seven sub-items as follows:

1. Market feasibility	:	It is defined as the extent of market demand for the product derived out of innovation and also the extent of scope for marketing the product.
2. Market stability	:	It is defined as the consistency of market price and demand of product derived out of innovation
3. Cost	:	This is of two types, initial cost and continuing cost. Initial cost represents the capital investment required for adoption of innovation. Further, the cash or inputs required for subsequent years use of innovation is termed as continuing cost.
4. Net profit	:	It is defined as the quantum of monetary benefit obtained by an individual through adoption of innovation.
5. Profit consistency	:	This denotes the regularity of net returns obtained by an individual or group of individuals over a period of time by adoption of an innovation.
6. Utility potential	:	It is defined as the degree to which the multiple use potential of an innovation to an individual or group of individuals through adoption of innovations.
7. Time saving	:	Indicates the best efficiency of an innovation in terms of saving time in different aspects.

B. Compatibility

Compatibility is the degree to which an innovation is consistent with past experiences, existing values, and future plans of the adopters. Compatibility is divided into seven sub-groups as follows:

1. Cultural compatibility : Is defined as the degree to which an innovation is consistent with the values and norms of the society.
2. Social compatibility : It denotes prestige gain or esteem by individual in the society through adoption of an innovation.
3. Physical compatibility : Is the degree to which an innovation is consistent and fit into the needs and interests of the adopters.
4. Pyschological compatibility : Is an innovation usefulness as perceived by the members of the social system.
5. Situational compatibility : Denotes the consistency and harmony of the innovation with previous practices followed by the adopters of innovation.
6. Relational compatibility : It is the degree to which an innovation can be adopted independently by the adopters just like other practices.
7. Anticipated compatibility : An innovation should be consistent with the future ideas of the adopter over a period of time.

C. Practicability

Practicability is the degree to which an innovation can be easily communicated, tested, demonstrated and practiced in the social system.

1. Point of origin	:	Indicates the credibility of the source from where the innovation originated.
2. Access to advise	:	For implementation of innovation, its extent of availability of original and detailed information for guidance and clearing doubts that arise while implementing it.
3. Visibility	:	Is the degree to which the results of an innovation are visible.
4. Trialability	:	Is the degree to which new idea can be tried on a small scale.
5. Mastery	:	Is the degree to which the practice of an innovation could be learned or mastered in a short period of time.
6. Demonstrability	:	It is the degree to which an innovation can be demonstrated to members of social system easily.
7. Communicability	:	Is the degree to which the information about the new idea can be diffused to members of the social system easily and speedily.

D. Complexity

Complexity is the degree to which an innovation is relatively difficult to understand and use.

1. Failure probability	:	It is the degree to which an innovation chances of failure and uncertainty of results after its adoption.
2. Discomfort saving	:	Represents avoidance of physical

		discomfort may be derived by adoption of an innovation.
3. Resource complexity	:	Is the degree of difficult in getting the necessary inputs and other resources for the application of an innovation.
4. Reversibility	:	It is the degree of ease with which the innovation can be replaced in case of its failure for adoption.
5. Work efficiency	:	Is the degree to which the adoption of new idea saves labour or increase the available labour efficiency.
6. Cognitive complexity	:	Is the degree to which an extent of relative difficult in understanding an innovation.
7. Application complexity	:	It is the relative difficulty of an innovations use and application on the farm.

Therefore, the possibility of a more sustainable productive technologies has to be tackled through agricultural research. Hence, agricultural universities and research stations should give due consideration for developing appropriate technologies to modernize Indian agriculture.

9

PRA AND FSR/E — TWO NEW APPROACHES FOR RURAL DEVELOPMENT

— *Madhab Adhikari* and *G.S Momi*

Since independence the foodgrain production in India has increased considerably. Starting from 50.82 million to tonnes during 1950-51, it has reached a staggering 203.54 m. tonnes during 1998-99. It is however to be noted that 75 per cent of the overall production is the contribution of eight States and of these eight States only three States contribute for 42 per cent of the overall foodgrain production (Economic Survey 1998-99). On the other hand there is a remarkable yield gap in case of rice, in the major rice growing States. Over a period of 7 years (1990-91 to 1997-98) the yield difference at all India level was 3022 kg/ha. (Survey of Indian Agriculture 2000). So such an erratic distribution in productivity clearly indicates that production technologies developed by our research institutes have not been totally adopted by our farming community. The population is also increasing while cultivable land is decreasing. With the fading glory of 'Green Revolution', there is an urgent need of increasing the productivity and diversify of our agriculture. So far there are three separate subsystems namely Research sub-system, Extension sub-system and ultimately User sub-system and there is little interrelationship between them. But the recent experience shows that all these sub-systems have to be conceived as the integrated holistic sub-systems each having a role to play at every stage. In serving the needy segment of the society lies the success of any development programme. To improve the economic condition of the rural mass we need to evolve suitable programmes and the farming community must have a say during the process of technology generation. Blanket recommendation of technology even for different areas have sometimes proved to be futile to the problems of the farmers in a particular area. So there is a strong need of individual system based research with the active participation of the farmers and that can only bridge the gap between farmers' choice and wisdom and the technology introduced by the outside agencies.

In this chapter two closely related approaches namely Participatory Rural Appraisal and Farming System Research and Extension have been discussed with a view to finding some alternatives for the inadequacy of traditions, disciplinary-oriented research strategies and the age old 'transfer of technology' models, which cannot withstand the test of time.

Farming Systems Research and Extension (FSR/E)

It is of utmost importance to understand the intricacies of socio-economic and ecological environment within which the resource poor farmers operate and to resolve their problems by collaborating with them according to their needs and priorities. It was to deal with this issue that the Farming Systems Research (FSR) was evolved in the 1960s whose objective was to further research in the area of farming systems, analyse problems and plan research and extension activities. It is an improvement over the conventional and essentially one-way model of technology generation and diffusion, which is from research station to extension agency to farmer. However, the long term success of FSR largely depends on the extent to which farmers are utilising the research output. It is in this context that the FSR methodology has to be integrated with technology diffusion. This concept of actively encouraging extension personnel to participate in FSR technology development is called the Farming Systems Research and Extension (FSR/E).

FSR/E is being developed as an approach to agricultural development in recognition of the 'inadequacy of the traditional disciplinary-oriented research strategies to solve the complex problem of small resource poor farmers working in less favourable natural environments' (NAARM, 1991).

Different opinions regarding FSR/E has become so much confusing that it indicates a set of research approaches rather than a specific methodology.

Merrill-Sands (1986) has suggested that atleast six different research activities can be recognised within this perspective. They are : (1) Farming system analysis, (2) Farming systems adaptive research, (3) Farming systems component research, (4) Farming systems base line data analysis, (5) New farming systems development, (6) Farming systems research and agricultural development.

Elements for FSR/E (Gibbon, 1991).

Although farming systems research approaches have developed through a variety of individuals, institutions and regions, there are a number of key elements that are, or should be, common to all. These are :

1. Farming systems research requires researchers to develop a holistic perspective of the real social, economic and political environment that is experienced by rural communities.
2. A specific client orientation is possible, following the study and identification of differentiated groups of farmers and user groups.
3. As most scientists are trained in one discipline, it is normally necessary to put together multi-disciplinary teams (natural and social scientists) for farming systems research to be effective.
4. Farming systems research is intended to focus on problems identified by and with farmers.
5. To be effective, farming systems research also should be well linked to other scientific programmes, which can provide

specific support and skills to extension agencies, planners and policy makers to solve particular problems.

6. One of the most important features of farming systems research is that it should develop in a dynamic, flexible way and continually respond to changing circumstances in an iterative manner.

Need for FSR/E

In India research in agriculture has been mostly on cropping systems as to the types and number of crops that could profitably be grown on a piece of land and the judicious combination of crops thereof and the consequent package of practices for exploiting the yield potential per unit area per unit time. With a plateau like situation developing in crop yield after the initial break through achieved and the emphasis on disversified agriculture, global market and liberalization of economy, the research has now to be diversified as well. Along with cropping system the agricultural research scenario now should be inclusive of all the allied activities like Dairy, Animal Husbandry, Fisheries, Poultry, Apiculture, Sericulture, Mushroom Culture and so on. All these sister enterprises have to be judiciously combined as a major enterprise for raising the income of the farm families. Suitable research and extension models will have to be developed for combining all these activities and a sound research programme to work on all these parameters simultaneously to generate technology modules to suit different locations and farmer typology is urgently required (Jha, 1999).

Limitations of FSR/E

1. Focus on farm household as a principal unit of analysis is not always appropriate.
2. Stages approach to FSR/E is not always appropriate.
3. Inadequate understanding and analysis of household differentiation, particularly with respect to gender.
4. Many farming systems are diverse, complex and uncontrollable

Participatory Rural Appraisal (PRA)

In the late 1970s a concept namely Rapid Rural Appraisal emerged which meant approaches and methods of enquiry about rural life and conditions which tried to offset the anti-poverty biases of Rural Development Tourism (the brief rural visit by the urban based professional) and to avoid the many defects of large questionnaire surveys. (Chambers, 1993). It was mainly influenced by the FSR. But there was a general trend among the outside agencies to consider themselves superior and so have behaved in ways which have almost universally inhibited the expression of local people's capabilities. So came the idea of Participatory Rural Appraisal (PRA). It is a continuing outgrowth of RRA. In the latter 1980s and in parallel the word 'participatory' was applied to RRA both in India through the work of Aga Khan Rural Support-programme with the International Institute for Environment and Development, London (McCacken,.1988).

Participatory Rural Appraisal is 'a family of approaches and methods to enable rural people to share, enhance and analyse their knowledge of life and conditions to plan and to act' (Mukherjee, 1995).

It is also called as the process of involving local people in the analysis and interpretation of a rural situation.

Principles of PRA

The principles of PRA after Chambers (1992) are :

- A reversal of learning i.e. learning from people.
- Learning rapidly and progressively with flexible use of methods, improvisation, iteration and cross checking.
- Offsetting biases, especially those of rural development tourism.
- Optimising trade offs, including principles of optimal ignorance.
- Triangulating, meaning using a range of methods, types of information etc.
- Seeking diversity i.e. seeking variability rather than averages.

- Facilitating–they do it.
- Self critical awareness and responsibility.
- Sharing of information and ideas between rural people, between them and facilitators and between different facilitators.

Mukherjee (1995) has also given the following principles :

- Increase involvement of local people.
- Learning from and sharing with the common people.
- Collecting as much information as is necessary to avoid getting into the problem of 'data diarrhoea' that is resorting to optimal ignorance..
- Exploring the range of circumstances.
- Investigating each issue at hand in different ways and from different perspectives.
- Ensuring involvement of people in the entire process.
- Adopting an informal approach.

Steps in use of PRA

PRA uses the general principles of programme planning but it is more people centered. The steps are as follows:

1. Select a particular village or area.
2. Conduct a priliminary visit.
3. Collect data using different tools of PRA.
4. Assist the community members in analysing the information they have collected through PRA.
5. Assist the community in identifying the issues/problems that affect the lives of most people.
6. Rank the opportunities.
7. Prepare a village resource management plan.
8. Help the community to search for resources outside the community.

9. Adoption and implementation of the plan by developing a clear agreement between the community, government and NGOs on their roles and responsibilities as also the time to be taken for each step.
10. Follow up and Evaluation
11. Dissemination of Findings

Strengths of PRA

Samanta (1992) has mentioned the following strengths of PRA:

Community forum : PRA provides an arena for the community to discuss its needs in a broadly based forum and strengthen dialogue among the community, government technical officers, NGOs, and other interested parties.

Local solutions: The process brings leaders of the communities together to find locally sustainable solutions to the communities needs.

Adequate data: PRA generates sufficient data for the community to rank problems and consider solutions, integrated with technical and economic considerations from government officers and NGOs.

Systematized participation : PRA provides a structure that makes it possible for individuals to identify how they could participate. It also serves as a catalyst for local and external elements to introduce positive change.

Accelerated changes already in motion : PRA mobilizes the community, accelerates forces already underway, and persuades technical officers, NGOs, and donor agencies that their communities are good for investments of time and development energies.

Builds self confidence : PRA enables villagers to achieve significant accomplishments in project activity.

Stimulates self reliance : The process creates a sense of

accomplishment as well as awareness that communities need not wait for government or donors to come before starting to solve community problems.

Limitations of PRA

Chambers (1992) has pointed out five dangers in the use of PRA. They are faddism (it can be discredited by over rapid adoption and misuse), rushing (too rapid), formalism, role (habit of routine) and rejection.

The limitations can also be pointed out in the following manner:

1. Changing the attitude of people is time-consuming and resource-intensive.
2. PRA methods are complementary to other research methods not supplementary.
3. Rapid appraisal may not always be appropriate for understanding composite social change.
4. Visual representations may sometimes be alien to many societies.
5. It may raise local expectation and thus need followup action.
6. PRA methods may not be cross culturally transferable.
7. Sensitive issues need to be handled carefully otherwise it may lead to exacerbating hybernating social tensions.
8. The initial enthusiasm may die easily.
9. For its success we need people's empowerment and participation friendly environment.

Conclusion

PRA and FSR/E are powerful methodology for rural development and it is important that their limitations are recognised and understood so as to bring maximum benefit to the society. In PRA, the people own more of the information in which they identify the priorities. Therefore for making rural development programmes effective and meaningful the PRA has to be considered as an important tool and implemented. This is high time that Farmer Participatory FSR/E should be widely accepted and adopted as the model of future Agricultural development by giving it a fair trial with all seriousness as a new plank of Agricultural Research and extension methodology for field relevance of technology generated and for wider acceptability by farmers of different socio-economic profile.

REFERENCES

Bheemappa, A. (1996). Participatory Rural Appraisal : Learning with the farming community: *Kurukshetra,* XLIV:S8-59.

Chambers, R. (1992). Rural Appraisal : Rapid, Relaxed and Participatory, IDS Discussion paper 311, IDS, Sunsex.

Chamber, R. (1993). *Challenging the Professions.* Intermediate Technology Publications Ltd. London.

Economic Survey 1998-99, Government of India.

Gibbon, D. (1991). The future of Farming systems research in developing countries. Proceeding of the National Workshop - Farming Systems Research in India: Strategies for implementation. NAARM, Hyderabad, India.

Jha, P.N. (1999). Farmer participatory farming system research/extension approach for making farm technology relevant to the field situation and for wider acceptability by farmers. Proceeding of National Workshop on Farmerled Participatory Extension, PAU, Ludhiana, Nov. 27-28, 1999.

McCracken, J.A. (1988). Participatory Rapid Rural Appraisal in Gujarat: (India), International Institute for Environment and Development, London.

Merrill-Sands, D. (1986). Farming System Research : Clarification of terms and concepts. *Experimental Agriculture,* 22 : 87-104.

Mikkelsen, B. (1995). *Methods for Development Work and Research : A guide for Practitoners.* Sage Publication, New Delhi.

Mukherjee, A. (1995). *Micro-level Planning for Rural Development in Participatory Framework : Application in Participatory Rural Appraisal* : Mukherjee A., Vikas Publishing House Pvt. Ltd., Delhi, pp. 20.

Mukherjee, N. (1998). *Participatory Rural Appraisal, Methodology and Applications.* Concept Publishing Company, New Delhi.

NAARM, 1991 Implications of FSR/E in the Indian Context : Theme papers, National Academy of Agricultural Research Management, Hyderabad, India.

Samanta, R.K. (1992). Participatory Rural Appraisal for purposive Development, *Kurukshetra,* XLI : 31-33.

Survey of Indian Agriculture, 2000, *The Hindu.*

10

FARMER PARTICIPATORY PLANT BREEDING

An Innovative Approach in Technology Generation

— *P. Arunachalam, R.Saravanan* and *N. Anandaraja*

Farmers participation is recommended for the development and promotion of new agricultural technologies to appropriately suit the farmers needs. Approaches derived from 'top down' centralized research proved inappropriate to farmers (Witcombe, 1999). Recent realization that farmers knowledge is equally valuable in earning the status of an equal partner in agriculture technology generation and dissemination. However, current plant breeding programmes are ignored to utilize farmers' knowledge of crops. To meet food security in near future, it is essential to increase the pressure on crop improvement programmes. The stagnation in food production is a prognostic to look forward for an alternative crop improvement approaches which fits to present needs. People participation places a vital role in all the development programmes. Crop breeding based on decentralised selection may still miss its objective if it does not utilize farmers' knowledge of crops and environment. The prime objective of participatory crop improvement programme acquires farmers' knowledge right from planning to development of cultivars. Decentralised selection is a powerful methodology to fit crops into the given physical (climate and management) environment.

Need for Farmers Participation in Technology Generation

- Conventional research has limitations
- Difficulty in achieving universality in agricultural research
- Farmers research has limitations
- Farmers possess creative abilities (Sethurao, 1998)

Top Down Approach

In spite of a large number of new high yielding varieties released through various crop improvement programmes, local varieties are also prevailing in many parts of the world. Such local types constitute an essential basis for advances in professional plant breeding which serve as a source of resistant genes for disease and pest, local adaption and, specialized grain qualities which is preferred by local people. The present approach has following lacuna:

- Current plant breeding programmes ignores to utilize the farmers' knowledge.
- The domains of released cultivars are defined inadequately.
- The Multi Location Trials (MLT) are carried out in different environment conducted by National co-ordinated trials. Even some trials are carried out in farmers' field where, differential response of genotypes (adaptability) to given environment are considered, irrespective of 'differential preference of genotypes but farmers (social adaptability) which vary from region to region.
- Multi location trials are usually conducted at high levels of inputs. But most of the farmers are resource poor and the majority of our cultivable areas comes under marginal and dry land. So the high yielding varieties may fail to perform to its actual potential (Joshi and Witcombe, 1996).

- All varieties/hybrids, that are released from different research stations have evolved from a handful of related genotypes.

Decentralised Approach

This decentralised approach demands participation of farming folk, to hull out the limitations of top-down approach, which insist the joint working of scientist and farmers to make crop improvement programmes practically and economically viable. The farmers traditional knowledge and experience are exploited right from planting/setting objectives, parental selection; selection preferred lines and adaption trials.

The farmers involved in crop improvement programmes by two ways, such as participatory varietal selection and participatory plant breeding. Participatory Varietal Selection (PVS) is followed to increase the adoption rate of improved varieties, which need to try a wide range of novel cultivars in the farmers' field through their involvement. In Participatory Plant Breeding (PPB) approach the farmers select their preferred line in breeding material. This concept is a logical extension of PVS. However, the first option should be PVS, since PPB is more resource consuming (Witcombe *el al.*, 1996). Therefore, PPB approach should be used only when the potential of PVS has already been exhausted. This participatory breeding can also exploit the cultivars identified through PVS for further crop improvement. The involvement of farmers from different regions is necessary to select their preferred genotypes, which are suitable to their preferential needs, specific agroclimatic situation and cropping pattern.

Farmers' participation approach in crop improvement programmes has following merits:

- Land races and locally adapted cultivars are commonly used as parents.
- Identification of suitable improved released cultivars to provide a large "basket of choices" (Chamber, 1989) for farmers.
- Farmer unacceptable genotypes are identified at early stage

itself, especially when quality traits are important.

- Farmers and their families assess all major parameters relevant to farmers, for example, taste, cooking quality, market value, and not just the limited set of characteristic measured in plant breeders trials.
- Participatory rural appraisal to identify the major characteristics of local land races. Cultivars obviously unacceptable for easily identified characteristics such as grain type, crop duration and plant height could be avoided.
- PPB is most suitable approach to develop cultivar with specific adaptation to marginal environments.
- Testing in the most appropriate environment – the farmer's fields with unchanged farmer management.
- Decentralised breeding would clearly define cultivars domains (Joshi and Witcombe, 1996).
- The cultivars produced by PPB is acceptable to farmers and increase the genetic diversity (Sthapit *el al.*, 1996).
- Farmers involvement in crop improvement programme facilitates early farmer to farmer spread of cultivars.

Participatory Crop Improvement Programmes

Participatory Rural Appraisal (PRA)

Participatory rural appraisal were conducted on the major characteristics of local cultivators. This was done through focussed group discussion, farm walks, matrix ranking and household questionnaires. A number of other PRA techniques were also employed.

Focussed Group Discussion (FGDs): In the introductory trials, the data were collected before and after harvest by means of focussed group discussion (FGDs) with all participating farmers on aspects of the crop including taste, market value, threshing characteristics and storability.

Farm Walks: Farm walks were organized for the participating farmers to visit each other's plots so that all the cultivar would be compared in the discussions.

Matrix ranking: Employing matrix ranking technique, local land races were assessed by ranking them for multiple races.

Household Questionnaires (HLQs): HLQs used to assess to household's perception of the variety in terms of post-harvest traits such as cooking quality and the market value of the grain (Joshi and Witcombe, 1996).

Stages of Participatory Varietal Evolution

- Participatory surveys to describe the varieties farmers are growing.
- A search and procurement process for suitable new varieties.
- Experimentation by farmers in their own field, with the new varieties (Witcombe, 1999).

The breeders (scientists) have realised the importance of the farmers' participation in plant breeding programmes. The programmes that are in progress are reviewed briefly below:

Decentralised selection (Selection in the target environment) had been used by ICARDA (International Centre for Agricultural Research in the Dry Areas) to avoid the risk of useful lines being discarded, because of their relatively poor performance at the experimental stations. ICARDA had implemented a participatory breeding project entitled as "Farmers participation and use of local knowledge in breeding barley for specific adaptation". This project was conducted at nine villages in Syria. It conducted that an additional advantage of participatory breeding is that, farmers rapidly adapt the breeding material to the corresponding changes in agronomic practices of the target environment (ICARDA report, 1998).

Group Approach for Locally Adapted and Sustainable Agriculture (GALASA) project being implemented at Palakkad district in Kerala. In this programme apart from other objectives of participatory crop management practices, the farmers participatory research focused on to evolve improved strains of popular varieties of the regions. For example, a red kernel variety of Ponmany is yet to evolve under this project (*KAU News*, 2000).

A rice variety Kalinga-III was first tested in 1993, in Farmer Managed Participatory Research (FAMPAR) trial (Joshi and Witcombe, 1996). Participatory varietal selection was a development project, carried out by the following firm; Krishi

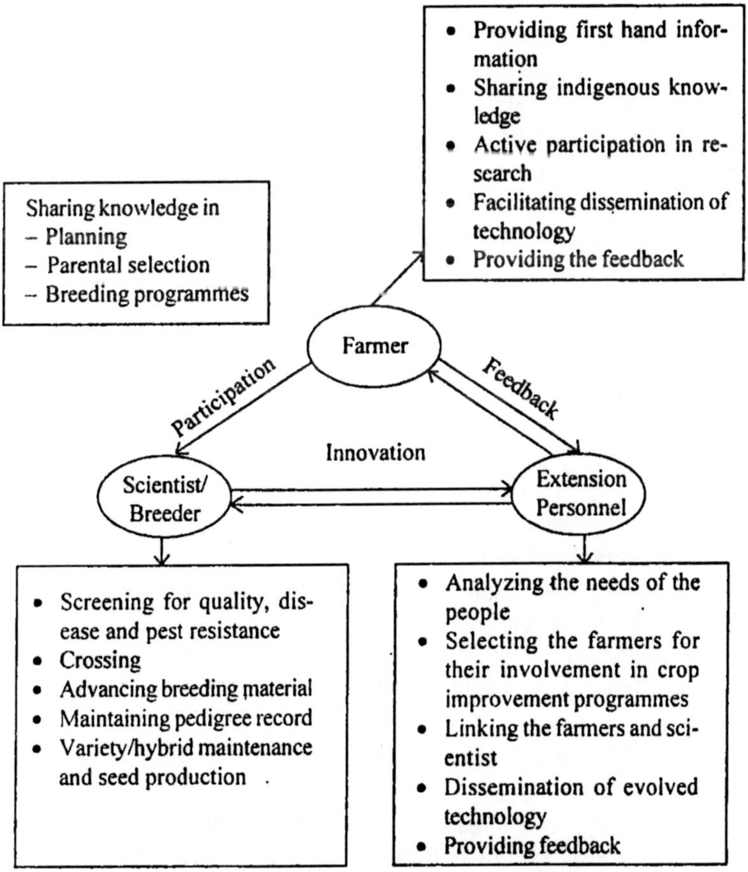

Model for Farmer Participatory Plant Breeding

Bharath Co-operative Ltd. (KRIBHCO) Indo-British Rain-fed farming Project (KRIBP) in western India. They showed that the rice (*Oryza sativa*) variety Kalinga-III was highly preferred by farmers (Witcombe *et al.*, 1999). They also stated that as a result of its rapid adoption, Kalinga-III was producing very high financial benefit. This vividly demonstrates the cost effectiveness of PVS, when highly preferred cultivars are identified.

Conclusion

Breeders and extension experts should draw a co-operative crop improvement programmes, which not only by way of inter-disciplinary approach but also through involving farmers to put the on-farm yield carve on an upward trend. The participatory crop improvement helps in rapid dissemination of cultivars through farmers-to-farmers contact, reducing cost of extension programmes in popularizing the cultivars. It is the right time to implement a various participatory breeding programmes, which not only meet the food security challenge and also reduce the cost of extension programme.

REFERENCES

Chambers, R., 1989. Institutions and practical change. In *Farmers First* (181-195) Eds. R. Chambers, A. Pacey and L.A. Thrupp, London, Intermediate Technology Publications.

ICARDA Report, 1998: Farmers preferences in Barley/Vetch rotation trials. *ICARDA Report*. pp. 5-6.

Joshi, A. and Witcombe, J.R. 1996. Farmer participatory crop improvement-II. Participatory varietal selection. a case study in India. *Exptl. Agric*. 32: 461-477.

KAU News, 2000. GALASA fields reap bumper crops. *KAU News*. I(2): 6.

Sethurao, M.K., 1998. Indigenous knowledge system and participatory technology development. Proceedings of National Seminar on *Participatory Technology Development*, Published by Kerala Horticultural Development Programme, Kochi.

Sthapit, B.R., Joshi, K.D. and Witcombe, J.R. 1996. Farmer participatory crop improvement-III. Participatory plant breeding, a case study for rice in Nepal. *Exptl. Agric.* 32: 479-496.

Witcombe, R. John, 1999. Do farmer participatory methods apply more to high potential areas than to marginal one's? *Outlook on Agriculture*, 28(1): 43-49.

Witcombe, J.R., Petre. R., Jones, S: and Joshi, A. 1999. Farmer participatory crop improvement-IV. The spread and impact of a rice variety identical by participatory varietal selection. *Exptl. Agric.* 35:471-487.

SECTION III : TECHNOLOGY DISSMINATION

11

CHANGING NEEDS OF EXTENSION DELIVERY SYSTEM

— P. Badrinarayanan

Extension Education as a means for transfer of technology among the client system (target groups) has undergone many changes in its approach mechanism for reaching greater speed and efficiency to transfer over the years. It is not merely the outcome of growing needs for greater volume of innovations to be passed on, their diversity and complexity, the increase in number and variety of clientele to be addressed and so forth but due to newer extension methodologies generated by extension exports themselves.

Diffusion and adoption pattern of innovations in agriculture have undergone a sea change from the days of Rogers and Shoemaker, who wrote their celebrated book on the subject laying down a "cross cultural approach". Training and Visit System of Extension and Broad based Agricultural Extension meant radical shifts in focus, from strengthening the skills of Extension Agency to that of extending the orbit of messages themselves.(Fig. 11.1).

Extension delivery has mainly been confined to Government Development Departments like Agriculture, Animal Husbandry, Cooperation etc. aimed primarily at rural clientele system, though Health and Family Welfare messages, Small Saving Campaigns etc. in urban areas also adopted Extension methodologies. Voluntary Agencies carrying on development activities in limited territory and major input agencies (fertilizer/cattle feed manufacturers etc.) also

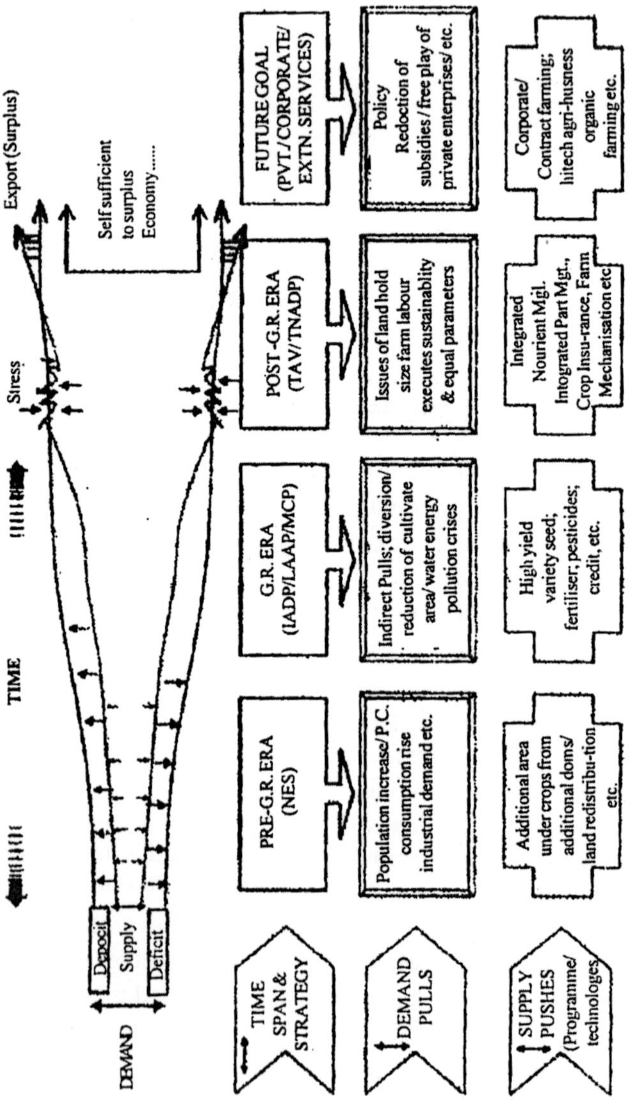

Fig. 11.1 : Diagrammatic Model of Agricultural Demand-Supply Dynamics

follow extension techniques, though a commercial rather than social motive is likely to dominate in the messages of input agencies.

A further dimension of contemporary extension significance is the change in clientele capacity, behaviour and expectations, wrought by increasing literacy levels, mass media impact and greater communication facilities (increased urban contacts) etc. that have changed the social dynamics in the rural side.

Extension Machinery carries the messages (innovations) generated by scientists. While scientists work on evolving techniques for solving problems of drought, pest, salinity, yield (by quality and quantity) and so forth, new problems relating to innovations themselves arise. The new problems are not necessarily restricted to the realm of production environment, but often extend beyond to encompass social, economic, regional, and even futuristic consequences of the innovations. This casts problems of resistance to be confronted by the extension machinery. Let us briefly consider a few instances of such controversial issues.

Hitech inputs and skills are criticised as directed towards richer clients for providing higher profits, thus widening the economic gap between rich and the poor, notwithstanding the host of low cost and no cost techniques identified for the poorer segment of farmers. Evolution of fertilizer responsive high yielding varieties were under such attack. A section of critics continue to share the view that science has made more economic chaos than other causes (inspite of host of studies and findings proving otherwise). Popular newspapers flash articles criticising scientific agriculture "Propagated by the Government" (the Extension Network) as intended to benefit industrial interests (Fertilizer/Pesticide factories) rather than the farming community. Such impressions carried by mass media pose obstacles to extension delivery.

Induction of labour saving farm machinery are the next much blamed subject. Mechanisation is reported to be throwing the poor rural workforce, particularly women, out of job. For example, the Paddy transplanter sought to be introduced in the delta districts, to reduce drudgery to the women planters as well as to speed up the planting, (particularly when the canal water is released late and massive area come under planting causing labour shortages, delayed planting and reduction in yields), was stoutly resisted by local interest groups, resulting in withdrawal of the programme itself. Host of skills provided to farm women to enhance their income through vegetable gardening, vermi composting, mushroom production etc., are not at all considered by these critics, who get much publicity and keep the extension in the need for constant defence of its well intended activities.

Abundance of superior grains (rice, wheat) production is blamed as the cause of decreased intake of millets, considered as nutritive grains, resulting in widespread deficiency among the rural poor. Rice-wheat tracts flourishing in irrigated domain have widened the economic gap between dry and irrigated tracts. The hybrid millets losing popularity due to extraordinary episodes (like green ear in cumbu) have also been projected as weaknesses of science, though they are miniscules compared to the abundance of problems solved by science. In the instant case, a whole gamut of factors like change of food habits among the ruralites on purely social grounds like easy cooking of rice (*vis-a-vis* millets, which require much processing before cooking), prestige factor in rice consumption, PDS coverage etc. are conveniently forgotten.

A more recent onslaught from a section of scientists themselves (who share the exaggerated anxieties of environmental and intellectual lobbies) relates to reduction of bio-diversity by man-made plant varieties and hybrids, the increasing extraction of vital resources (water, energy) and progressive degradation of cultivable land due to agro-chemical inputs, posing issues of sustainability, inter-generational equity etc. The IPM and INM approaches already launched by agricultural scientists and being promoted by the extension workers are somehow not appreciated by the critics.

Apart from the above message related issues there are criticisms on the extension delivery techniques as well:

- That extension is depending more on providing subsidy incentives for motivating adoption of innovations, rather than effective education, inducing spontaneous adoption.
- That subsidy incentives resorted by the extension create a dependency syndrome among the clients, who start looking

for some assistance or other for carrying out every good innovation.

- That demonstrations and trainings continue to be individualistic (Particular crop or subject oriented) rather than wholistic.
- That extension activities are more programme oriented to achieve the targets assigned at macro levels, rather than problem-oriented, to achieve local need based activities.
- That extension services are availed more by local pressure groups, rather than the large mass of poor farmers, and so forth.

In the backdrop of the above scenario of changes and emerging challenges in the way of our development mandates like achieving economic prosperity, ecological security and equity (social/regional/gender/etc.) the Extension Delivery System needs a thorough relook into the adequacy of its own mechanism to cope with the daunting tasks ahead and devise improvements.

As the subject is vast, varied and complex, it is felt expedient to restrict the discussion to a few critical issues bearing on the basics of the delivery system, in this article.

The Clientele Expectations
The Challenges to Production Environment
Problems in Extension Delivery.

(a) **Clientele Expectations**

The major expectations of an average modern farmer are:

(i) Cost effective techniques for higher productivity,
(ii) Assistance for farm mechanisation, considering acute shortage of farm labour and draught animals, during peak seasons,
(iii) Assured minimum price for the farm produce, and
(iv) Comprehensive risk cover against unforeseen crop losses by flood, drought, pests, etc.

There are indeed good techniques like micro irrigation (drip system), windmill water lifts (along coasts) etc. which are costly and need massive subsidy back-up for promotion, under small farm environments.

However, farm scientists have generated technologies for crop production suited to the small farm environment, which have also paid rich dividends in terms of reaching higher productivity in the predominantly small and marginal land holds of Tamil Nadu. In fact an IFPRI study of early 80's had clearly dispelled popular myths against Green Revolution technologies as favouring big farmers and widening the economic gap between small and big farmers. The international study conducted in the North Arcot district. (now bifurcated into Vellore and Thiruvannamalai) clearly upheld the benefits of G.R. technologies as neutral to farm hold size, with greater Small Farmers reaping benefits and the spread effect seen in the betterment of farm labourers as well. Emerging bio-fertilizer/biocide technologies are likely to further prove cost-effective, eco-friendly and enhance produce quality (not merely quantity) in the days ahead.

The availability of farm machinery suited to small farm environment like power tillers and small tractors (upto 30 hp) etc. have ushered in scope for timely field operations, efficiently and cost effectively. The investment assistance provided by credit institutions (carrying prescribed credit flow to agricultural sector) and subsidies provided by Government have encouraged mechanisation in recent years. However, the demand is growing while Government incentives are restricted deliberately, to slow down the pace of growth, in pursuance of the energy policies to keep the growing dependence on non-renewable fossil fuels under check. If more renewable sources (wind solar) come into play for operating farm machinery, the pace of mechanisation can be improved.

We have also to strike a note of anxiety that credit procedures adopted by financial institutions in the wake of liberalised procedures (that empowers Financial institutions to decide the level of security) had put whole lot of small farmers at much disadvantage in getting credit assistance for farm machinery, even at subsidised rates. The "viability" factor considered by banks (credit worthiness) in calling for 6 to 8 acres of assured irrigated land for sanction of loans for small tractors, is disputed by a section of bankers themselves who testify that a small farmer hiring his small tractor during peak seasons, is more regular in paying off loan, than a medium or big farmer who uses it solely for his own farm and often turns into a defaulter! These "extraneous" factors also affect adoption of viable techniques like mechanisation of farms, in the wake of labour and animal scarcity in peak (rainy) seasons.

Government is presently declaring Statutory Minimum Price for select farm produce, which is felt inadequate by the farming community in view of increasing input costs, wages, lease rent and so forth. The market interventions through monopoly procurement of paddy (Cauvery delta districts) prevent exploitative trade practices in a glut market. Parallel procurement is also resorted in surrounding districts to provide a reasonable price for the growers. However there is a limit to which Government itself can go for protecting the farmers. However, there is a limit to which Government itself can go for protecting the farmers. The right organisational strength is lacking in the farm community, as evident from the functioning of Regulated Markets. The recent programme of Farmers Shandy's for marketing perishables is holding some promise, due to strict monitoring and regulation (farmer's identity cadre) by Government Departments. Such external supports to protect farmer interests may not endure and dedicated organisations have to develop from the stakeholder group itself.

There is a further view shared even by elite agricultural experts that agriculture should be declared as industry. Induction of exotic perceptions into Indian rural scene, without considering our domestic susceptibilities, is causing genuine concern among seasoned extension workers familiar with our strengthen and weaknesses. Industrial status may bring some elite incentives. but deprive great deal of supports as well. The balance sheets have to be struck carefully, since a critical transition from abundance to reducing resources (by quantity and quality of water, land, power, labour, etc.) in production environment is going on.

Emergence of corporate/contract farming should involve local manpower, *not* merely in wage employment, but also in profit-sharing. Else, social equity may suffer serious setback. Also, *commercial interests may overlook social/ecological consequences, putting the efforts of 5 decades of extension to historic waste.* Extension experts should raise their voice above economic/elitist views, to preserve the rights and interests of the average farmer. Consider large extent of food crops converted to commercial crops earning millions of dollars and importing food at global rates! Either the poor will spend great portion of their increased wages (got from corporate farms) for food, or beg the Government to increase the Public distribution system budget! Also the commercial extension will rule the corporate farms and committed (Government) extension lose its (small farm) clients. In such a scenario, pressures of power centres rather than principles of equity would influence decisions of rural institutions (PRIs). Futuristic strategies have therefore to be generated by extension experts now.

Losses to farmers caused by natural hazards are covered under Crop Insurance under a programme jointly implemented by the Centre and the State. The scheme that covered farmers availing crop loans through cooperatives, has recently been extended to benefit non-loanees as well. The coverage of crops, risks and insurance levels have also been widened. But the rates of premium worked with reference to risk factors (for instance, more premium rate for rainfed than irrigated cotton), the method of loss estimation an area approach (block/panchayat basis) rather than on individual farm level basis, etc. are sure to be unattractive in farmer's eye. The high level of indemnity paid (more than premium collected), low service charges paid to banks, problems of inter-department coordination (Departments of Agriculture/Horticulture/Sugar/Cooperative/Statistics/etc.) are likely to irk the insurance people. But Govt. of India has already made it known that District/State/National level committees shall monitor and suggest measures for improving services; that global reinsurance shall be arranged to safeguard interest of insurance agency, etc. the expectations of farmers are therefore likely to be fulfilled in a great measures in the years to come.

(b) Challenges to Production Environment

Cultivable land

Progressive urbanisation and growth of industries are causing reduction of cultivable area and the Extension Worker has to work with lesser and lesser area under cultivation, to reach higher and higher productivity for meeting the galloping demands of the population and agro industries.

Government took some measures for curbing indiscriminate conversion of wet lands for house-site/industrial purposes, which has been sued and got quashed by High Court, on procedural grounds. Government is now examining appropriate enactments to preserve cultivable lands. In a developing economy shifts in land use pattern cannot be stopped, but measures to improve wasteland corresponding to the area of cultivable land diverted to non-agricultural purpose, has to be ensured. How this would be accomplished have to be explored.

Irrigation Water

Water is a renewable resource which nature through rains recycles for our use. Rain water is greatly pure (except in highly industrial territories with high sulphur dioxide level in atmosphere, where even acid rains may pour) and by proper harvest of water much benefit has been derived under Watershed Development Programmes. These efforts have to be intensified, in view of reducing storages in tanks caused by large-scale encroachments of catchments etc. That is why the saying, "Poverty is the worst pollutant" came into vogue, globally. Increasing demands of water for civic and industrial needs, reducing supplies from surface and underground sources, deteriorating quality caused primarily by urban and industrial effluents, inadequate energy for drawal of groundwater, particularly in summer when rivers and tanks are dry, costly alternatives for saving irrigation water (drip/biwall etc.) and a host of factors pose challenges for the future of irrigated agriculture.

Workforce

As the pace of urbanisation is gaining momentum rural farm force are drawn towards urban areas carrying lucrative wages. Greater mechanisation of farm activities would soon become a necessity. Initially farm machineries suited to small farm environment are likely to be in demand and the anticipated emergence of corporate farming would invite need for giant farm machineries. While talking of mechanisation, we have to feel sorry that local artisans who made the ploughs and share points, the harrows and the sickles shall be deprived of work. Even small machineries are now made in big factories at low cost, to benefit the farmer. But local carpenters and smiths have atleast to be trained in repair of these machineries, to earn their living. This is well within the purview of agricultural extention workers, who should propose such trainings through his own department, the DRDAs, NGOs and so forth.

Investment

Scope for greater returns on investment particularly from hi-tech agriculture, would call for massive skill upgradation among farming population to acquire latest know-how and do-how. Economists say that Government investment (including public sector organisations) in agricultural infrastructure is coming down, obviously due to compelling demands of more profitable sectors. But more overt reasons like maintaining costly irrigation structures, against indiscriminate encroachments and deliberate maldistribution by local interests themselves scares investment. Agro-processing ventures (e.g. sunflower oil plants) are also proving less remunerative against imported products that rule the market. Giant machineries abroad are able to process oil cheaply and compete in less developed countries. The result is a weak forward linkage, low farm gate price and shy technology adoption. Hence extension has a concern on all these aspects bearing on client behaviour. However expanding market opportunities opened by liberal economic policies, greater scope for agri-exports etc. shall throw open rich possibilities of market tie-up from business/industrial houses, with producers. However, investment-return relationships being wide and varied in hi-tech agriculture, commercial advantages rather than social necessities are likely to rule farm investments patterns calling for Government intervention to protect social interests.

We can list a whole range of such factors bearing upon farm production and the continuous need to bring viable adjustments to stall the adverse impacts and achieve higher income at farm level, food security at social level and economic prosperity at national level.

(c) **Problems in Extension Delivery**

There are divergent views regarding the performance of agricultural extension that implements agricultural development plans. An English sociologist says that in Third World countries, the national plans for development are influenced by international aid and commercial banking agencies giving capital. Donor views on local "problems of development" are influenced by their experience in their own countries. Their modernisation plans lead to dependency lending to the view, "aid creates more problems that it solves", etc. the continued poverty and indebtedness of Latin American countries pampered by western donors are usually cited as example of failure of aided programmes. Though we have had our own plans and objectives, the play of donor views on aided development programmes are not ruled out by the cities. In fact a former Director of the Centre for Development Studies, Chandigarh (Deep & Deep Publishers, New Delhi, 1991) says that chinese rural areas are well-developed in contrast to Indian urban bias. But Indian Agriculture has not failed by any count. We had reached self sufficiency and are working towards greater progress. Yet warnings are being struck by various quarters, both from within and outside the country.

The increased literacy levels in the rural side, the spell of urban influence, growth of private commercial input agencies and service centres, the changed rural leadership pattern etc. have greatly affected the adequacy of extension delivery. Let us consider a few issues affecting extension performance.

Extension education is facing tough challenges in the face of aggressive propaganda from commercial interests, which successfully incite people against extension messages on input regimes in order to push their own products and prescriptions. As extension services are free, its massive cheap inputs (subsidised) lack the glamour of commercial publicity and the messages are simple and straight rather than propagandist (propaganda being the anti-thesis of education), the people fail to appreciate extension services and the latter have to take aggressive measures to offset exaggerated commercial messages and vindicate the credibility of extension.

Extension functions are generally restricted to delivery of a few critical inputs and advisory services carrying some motivational incentives. The credit, power supply, fixation of minimum wages, tenancy policies and umpteen other needs of farmers lie outside the purview of Agricultural Extension System, making it helpless to ensure holistic support for farm production activities.

The rural social dynamics has deteriorated due to narrow groupist interests, dividing the people in the name of religion/ language/class and castes. Traditional leadership pattern has vanished and multiple leadership often conflicting among themselves have emerged, making it difficult to enlist their services in Extension. Several studies have indicated that factionalism in village and vested interests have played down good projects (Rajagopalan *et al.* and Narayana Reddy). The weak linkages among the various institutions serving agriculture, the diversity and enormity of activities taken up by the extension functionaries, stagnation in the career advancements of the Extension Workers have all contributed to significant erosion of efficiency in the Extension Delivery System.

Government is finding it costly to maintain its development administration particularly the staff costs. The decision to disperse its activities among Voluntary Agencies, private trade and people's institutions (SHGs/WUOs/etc.) have been taken as early as Eighth Five Year Plan itself. The pace of privatisation and co-operatisation of development activities with corresponding reduction in public services are likely to gain momentum in the Tenth Five Year Plan.

Accountability and output guarantee have been suggested to

justify extension outlays in recent years (though even commercial Public Sector Bodies do not provide any such guarantee at present). Yet, Extension network has the energy and expertise to guarantee reasonably pitched levels of production performance, regardless of availability or otherwise of subsidies and uncertain biotic influences. Just some guarantees on crucial issues like adequate and timely power supplies, credit flow, tie-up with market etc. could be secured in support of Extension.

The foresight of Alvin Toffier ("Future Shock") that bureaucracy would make way for adhocracy is already coming true. Extension is the ultimate answer to development either within or outside the Government. The Extension Machinery has to broaden its role from one of executor of Government programmes to generator of local, Production Programmes involving Government outlays, local NGO services, people's organisations etc. in a holistic way. The impressive impacts achieved would amply justify the Extension Investment, besides opening the gates of prosperity in the rural side and the country at large.

REFERENCES

Hazell, Peter B.R., C. Ramasamy, *The Green Revolution Reconsidered — The Impact of High Yielding Rice Varieties in South India.* Oxford University Press, First Indian Impression, 1993.

Rajagopalan, C.; Jaspal Singh, *Adoption of Agrl. Innovations — A Sociological Study of Indo German Project, Mandi.* National Publication House, Delhi, 1971.

Reddy, G. Narayana. Decision-making and Community Action. An Empirical Study". *Journal of Rural Development,* January, 1989.

Singh. S.N.,Vijayaraghavan. K., Heque. T.. *Transfer of Technology to Small Farmers — An Analysis of Constraints and Experiences.* Concept Publishing Company, New Delhi, 1991.

Webster, Andrew. *Introduction to the Sociology of Development.* Macmillan Education Ltd., London (II Edition) 1990.

12

SHGs : A Key to Technology Dissemination

— *K.J. Sherin* and *Shibu Sebastian*

Kerala Horticulture Development Programme was initiated in 1993 in order to lend a helping hand to the homestead and marginal farmers, were high cost of production has affected cultivation of fruits and vegetables.

The Important Support Lent to the Farmers are :

1. Planting materials are supplied at subsidised rates
2. Skill Development
3. Credit
4. Crop Insurance
5. Marketing
6. Post-harvest handling
7. Extension support
8. Research and Development
9. Value addition

The programme has maintained success so far by emphasizing on farmer participation in all stages. And this has been possible by the group approach as "Self Help Groups" (SHGs). Today over 1000 vegetable and 500 fruit growing SHGs are in existence. Each SHG consists of 5 to 20 farmers.

One of the key approaches used in the programme is the "Participatory Technology Development".

Participatory Technology Development (PTD) refers to enabling the farmers to develop and manage their own technology.

Objectives of PTD

(a) Enabling rural farming communities to meet their felt needs through farmer centred methods.

(b) Empower individual farmers and farming communities to assume responsibilities for the process of generation and adoption of technologies.

(c) Enhance farmers capacity to develop sustainable farming systems.

(d) Increase people's competence to identify their own needs, problems, threats and opportunities.

Features of PTD

1. People centred
2. Need based
3. Site specific
4. Wholistic
5. Farmer's resource based
6. Quicker diffusion

Role of Change Agents in PTD

1. Create enthusiasm
2. Ensure constructive participation
3. Involve people in planning and implementations
4. Respect farmer's culture and traditions
5. Start small and simple
6. Do not try to meet all needs at the same time

Based on the above, a study was conducted in Palakkad, Ernakulam and Trichur districts of Kerala. Over 60 farmers were identified representing 60 SHGs.

Findings of the study are classified as :

Strengthens

1. An SHG initiated in an area helps in establishing other SHGs in the same area.
2. The level of interest in order to know about new crops, scientific technologies has shown a steep increase among farmers.
3. Farmers who are non-members of SHGs are constantly keeping in touch with SHG farmers in order to know about new technologies, new crops, pesticides, fungicides, support systems, marketing etc.
4. The farmers have developed a sense of confidence in the programme and large number of farmers are taking up land for lease to cultivate crops.
5. Large tracts of paddy lands which were fallow are now used for banana and vegetable cultivation.
6. Farmers are willing to take up the advice given by KHDP in crop cultivation practices, a confidence which they had lost in Krishi Bhavan's.
7. Farmers are happy with the group marketing strategies followed, which saves upto Rs. 20/100 on their product.
8. The introduction of the farmers 'market concept' has increased the bargaining power of farmers.
9. Loans are available at the right time and required amount via KHDP which was not possible earlier, Banks are coming forward to provide loans to SHGs, as the repayment of loans is over 90 per cent. This has been possible due to peer pressure and monitoring by Master farmers.
10. Large number of farmers are ready to try out experiments on various crops in their fields.
11. Soil testing has been strictly adopted by farmers so as to avoid

over use of fertilizers and unwanted use of other fertilizers.

12. Large number of non-members sell their produce at the KHDP market to get the market price.
13. Farmers are able to receive inputs like seeds, fertilizers, pesticides and fungicides at subsidised or factory prices.
14. Free of any political or caste bias.
15. Better awareness and confidence by interacting with a large number of people.
16. KHDP has become the venue where farmers' needs, ideas are taken into account in making decisions and plans.

Weaknesses

1. People are not always willing to abide to the group approach.
2. Farmers giving more importance to loans, insurance etc.
3. Farmers consider many technologies developed by the Agricultural Universities and Agricultural Department Programmes are not need based and their exist a high level of corruption, politics etc.
4. Many farmers are self centred.
5. As the programme is area specific, highly skilled personnel are required
6. Maintenance and training costs are high

Conclusion

KHDP has taken a step as how agriculture can be made viable and feasible with farmer's participation. The technologies and concepts used can be adopted and replicated in other States taking into account the existing conditions in that area.

13

MODERNIZING INDIAN AGRICULTURE
Through Modern Technology Dissemination

— *N.K. Khare* and *Rajula Chandran*

India has successfully met the food requirements of millions of ever-growing population, which has crossed one billion mark recently. The growth of foodgrain production has crossed 206 million tonnes mark now. Thanks to the planners, administrators scientists, extensionists and above all our farming communities who have been putting continuous efforts to raise production and productivity of crops and thinking to exports foodgrains, vegetables, milk products and many agro-based products.

We have not to be complacent; we have to focus our efforts looking to the needs and challenges of 21st Century in terms of growing population and its requirements. The share requires 270 MT – foodgrain in 2010 – a gross increase of 35 per cent as projected. To realize the dream, we have to move beyond the confines of green revolution during 20th Century into the relive of all green and ever green revolution just waiting to unfold into 21st Century.

Modernizing agriculture for 21st Century in which four basic systems. i.e. Technology development, technology dissemination, technology utilization and nature policies and strategies. This chapter presents the modern information technology dissemination needed for modernizing agriculture in India in 21st century.

Modernization refers to the state of society like traditional, transistful and modernized society. It has a set of goals and it provides a set of agenda for action and its refers to the process movement and take account the GNP and degree of industrialization.

Nature of Modernization

It is revolutionary process
It is complex and multidimensional
It is systematic process
It is lengthy process
It is phased process
It is irreversible process
It is progressive process
It is global process
It is homogenize process or global village

Significance of Farm Information

We are living in the "Information Age." Information is a vast dynamic and inexhaustible source that affects all disciplines as well as the lives of all people. Agriculture and technology are no exception. Information in Agriculture is used to support research and development for the production of foods and services that touch all our lives and it can be used to improve the quality of life. The rapid strides made in Information Technology (IT) in recent years have encouraged many development communicators to extend its benefits to agricultural and rural development. It is the universal truth that access to information holds the key for successfully development and same dedicated and enterprising scientists and technologists are making their best efforts to take the benefits of the IT revolution to the rural poor. The IT that computerized communications will fundamentally change the world. It is a powerful tool that will help accelerate the development process. It has been proved beyond doubt that this technology favours small users. Given the necessary support and education, it will surely lead the way to a brighter tomorrow in the rural sector.

According to IT experts, "Unit recently, telecommunications was considered a luxury to be provided only after investment in water, electrification and roads had been made – and after all the demand for telecommunications in the cities had been met. Instead, it should be considered a vital component in the development process – a complement to other development investments – that can improve the productivity and efficiency of rural agriculture, industries and social services and can enhance the quality of life in developing regions".

The use of computers in agriculture is well-established in developing countries. The Internet and other forms of computer networking can be useful for exchanging market information with the growers (Venkataramani, 1999).

The overall size of national Agricultural Basket would grow around 60 per cent by 2010. It includes foodgrains, animal and agro-industry based and horticultural produce. Population size may grow by 20 per cent by then. Thus, aggregate availability from this composite basket to each family is going to be fairly comfortable– say 33 per cent more than what it is today. However, the dream of the nation's policy makers to double the Agricultural Production by 2010 is likely to fall short by 40 per cent mark. To realize the dream, we have to move beyond the confines of green revolution witnessed during 20th century into the realm of all green and ever green revolution just waiting to unfold into 21st century (Goel, 2000).

Present Day Extension Role

The extension is now becoming more diversified, more technology intensive and more demand driven. This requires the Extension Worker at the cutting edge level to be master of so many trades, which is well nigh impossible. The use of IT will help the extension workers to be more effective in meeting farmers information needs. It is going to play a pivotal role in extending Agriculture extension service more effectively to farmers. It is now possible to furnish the latest information to farmers by developing an interactive multimedia for finding solution to various problems facing by farmers at different stages of their farming operations.

Access to information and improved communication is a crucial requirement for sustainable agricultural development in 21st century. Modern communication technologies when applied to conditions in rural areas can help improve communication, increase participation, and disseminate information and share knowledge and skills. It is said that we live in the information Age. We are surrounded and constantly bombarded by information-related technology. It is also said that technology will change the world. Historians, however, testify that technology does not change the world, but the people who adopt and use technology make the changes. For effective change, timely, integrated and good quality communication of information is needed. By definition, effective communication is a two way process. Communication. is an interactive process. In this age of information computer based multimedia technology is a tool for communicators of all trades and an effective catalyst for change.. The computer application in Extension will the be major form of technology dissemination in future. Some of them are calling "Cyber Extension". The advent of INTERNET on communication scenario offers enormous potential for two-way on-line communication between distant parties via the telecommunication and computer network spread over the entire globe. The world is rapidly shrinking to a global village. The merger of communication (audio and video) and computer technology has made this combination so powerful that no sector of human activity can afford to ignore it.

Improved communication and information access is directly related to social and economic development. There is a concern that the gap between the information rich and information poor is getting wider. New information and communication technologies are generating possibilities to solve problems of rural poverty, inequality, and giving an opportunity to bridge the gap between information rich and information poor and support sustainable development in rural and agricultural communities. The ongoing IT revolution has opened huge opportunities for providing access to information as well as to interactive distance learning in rural India. Computer aided knowledge dissemination mechanism help to reach the un-reached and foster new voices and new leaders. Any kind of effort in this direction will be highly effective way to empower the rural population with the most needed commodity i.e. INFORMATION.

Looking to the statistics of Internet subscriber's base of Videsh Sanchar Nigam Limited (VSNL) increased from 4151 in 1995-96 to 213,048 in 1998-99. In 1998-99 alone the total subscriber's base in the country has grown over 185 per cent to 2,54,000 till March 1999, added by opening up of this to private players. INFAC projections indicate that Internet subscriber's base would grow at compound annual growth rate (CAGR) of about 110 per cent to reach 1.75 million in 2002-03 (Sharma, 2000).

The constitution of IT Task Force by Government of India and subsequent acceptance of its main recommendations is a very positive step in this direction of agriculture. (Recommendation no.79). "The government shall take all necessary steps to boost IT for Agriculture and integrated rural development. Towards this end, a number of demonstration project will be devised in each State taking into account the specific strengths and needs at local level. A unique "wired village" pilot project has been launched under the aegis of National Information Technology Task Force at Warna Nagar, Kolhapur district in Maharashtra. Efforts will be made to quickly replicate such projects in other States."

There are cases of application of information and communication technologies that have made difference in the delivery of services in rural India. Some of these include – Warna Wired Village Project, Information Villages Project, Milk Collection in Dairy Cooperatives (NDDB), Information Technology Application for Indian Rural Postal System (CMS Ltd.), Knowledge Network for Grassroots Innovations (IIM), Application of Satellite Communication for Training Field Workers and Extension Workers in Rural Areas (ISRO's), Computerization of Mandal Revenue Offices (MRO's) and Computer Aided Administration of Registration Department in A.P. (Sharma 2000).

Modern Information Dissemination Technology

The traditional extension methods are expensive, time consuming, quality of message distorted as it passes through different channels, poor quality of communication by extension personnel. Thus we can say the traditional extension methods are very limited, and can not reach in all the villages and all the farmers. The research pointed out that farmers are more dependent on other than public extension system for getting technical advice as well as farming inputs. (Sharma 2000).

G-7 Ministerial Conference on Information Society (1995) concluded that the:

- Information and communication technology and services can make an important contribution to sustainable development in all the countries of the world.
- The information infrastructure in the less industrialized area of the world is limited.
- Developing the information infrastructure can prevent an increase in economic and social disparities.
- The needs of developing countries are often very different from those of more industrialized nation.
- Developing countries must develop strategies for entering the global information society geared to their needs and realities.

The information society is expected to deliver for reaching positive change in very sphere of our lives; improvements in education and health care systems the harnessing of human resources, effective public administrations and services (Geraled Lange, 1998).

Sharma, (2000) more emphasised on IT and given the term "Cyber Extension". Cyber Space is the imaginary or Virtual space of computers connected with each other on Networks, across the globe. These computers can access information in form of Text,

Graphics, Audio, Video and Animation file. Software tools on network provide facilities to interactively access the information from connected services. Thus, cyber space can be defined as imaginary space behind the interconnected telecommunications and computer networks the virtual world.

Cyber Extension means "using the power of online networks, computer communication and digital interactive multimedia to facilitate dissemination of Agricultural. technology". It include effective loss of information and communication technology, national and international information Networks, Internet, Expert Systems, Multimedia Learning System and Computer Based Training System to improve information access to the Farmers, Extension Workers, Research Scientists and Extension Managers.

Mishra 1999 defined cyber extension as extension over cyberspace, the imaginary space behind the inter-connected telecommunication and computer networks, the virtual world.

Advantages of Computer Based Information Technology

1. Computer Based Information Technology will save many time and efforts–Scientists will prepare electronic version of messages themselves. These versions do not have to be printed and posted. This process will have time and money. The messages will be updated online and that save time too. This can provide more in-depth analysis and can also provide detail on farm research results to the ultimate users.
2. Computer Based Information Technology will save time, cut steps from extension process – Computer Based Information Technology will cut a number of steps altogether from the traditional extension process. In agriculture, zonal workshop, training to subject matter specialist etc. can be eliminated. All the concerned will get the information immediately and queries/ clarifications will also be addressed equally fast, without involving a chain of extension machinery.
3. Computer Based Information Technology will be information rich and interactive. It appeals to the curious extension workers and analytical farmers. It will allow them to search and locate

the information they need quickly. The extension worker can talk to the concern scientists for more information on the subject, wherever the scientists may be. The rural technologies can be made available on CD-ROMs for quicker dissemination.

4. Computer Based Information Technology offers instant international reach – Online networks have created an instant global village. It will eliminate the time and distance barrier that get in the way of knowing the latest information on any particular problem from any part of the world.

5. Computer Based Information Technology will be continuously available – One of the key attributes of an online information service is that it is available all the time, 24 hours a day, 365 days a year. Computer Based Information Technology does not sleep, he doesn't go on leave. If you have connectivity you can get information, from wherever it is available.

Now it is the job of scientists particularly the extension professionals to collate, edit and package the technical information and put it on the net. The national, regional and State level institutes like IARI/NIRD/MANAGIE/SIRD's/ KVK's/ ZRS/SAU's/ Mandis have a very important role to play in taking lead to package the information on Agricultural Extension and Rural Development Policies, Schemes, programmes and working mechanism at the grass-root level and host the same on their WEB sites. To meet the challenges of 21st Century we need to facilitate the task of taking information access to the village level. There is already a concern that the gap between the information rich and information poor is getting wider. Hence, it is incumbent on all of us, the administrators, NGO's, trainers, extension workers and scientists, all who are for upliftment of the rural communities to provide information access to the last person in the rural areas; reaching the un-reached.

The Important Tools of Computer Based Information Technology

1. E-mail
2. Telnet

3. FTP
4. Gopher, Archie, Veronica
5. Usenet Newsgroups
6. World Wide Web.

1. *Electronic Mail*

A further dimension opened up when file transfer for communication purpose became possible. E-mail rose to prominence by emulating the structure of the conventional postal system, with "electronic mail boxes", as servers and personal "mail readers" are clients. Now-a-day's E-mail is the most frequently used application by the Scientists, Extension Workers. Currently, over 50 million people using for business and personal use. E-mail allows us to send and receive text messages to other users of the Internet. For many people e-mail is the only Internet application used. E-mail can be send/read using a number of tools. Some are free programmes, some are free and some are shareware. Some of the well known e-mail tools are Web Browser like Netscape, Internet Explorer etc., Lotus Notes, Endora etc. E-mail address are of the syntax: mailbox @ domain. To send an e-mail you have to know the receiver's e-mail address.

2. *Telnet*

Telnet is an application that allows you to log on to a remote computer. It is like a terminal emulation programme. Telnet session's present text based data as a terminal would. However, now Graphic User Interface Clients are now available which offer better service.

3. *File Transfer Protocol (FTP)*

FTP use to send copies of files from one computer to another and responsible for highest percentage of data transferred on Internet.

4. *Gopher, Archie, Veronica*

Gopher was the first attempt of making it easy to access resources on the Internet. Till 1994 Gopher was considered the most useful Internet tool. This uses text based nested menus to access FTP sites, directories, files and documents. The University of Minnesota's gopher system was the first milestone. Archie, Veronica, Jughead, and other sites were all developed to assist with finding the right Gopher site. Gopher transactions, and in fact a user is offered link to Gopher site without realizing it. The information available on a gopher server is presented in a hierarchical menu modelled on the basic structure of files and directories.

5. *Usenet Newsgroups*

Newsgroups provide bulletin board type area where user can read other opinions and are sent entries of their own to be posted. Modern web browsers like Netscape and Explorer include software for reading and posting to Usenet. E-mail mailing lists are an alternative for Usenet groups at these lists are normally more focussed.

6. *World Wide Web (WWW)*

The WWW system was being developed at CERN in Europe. The World Wide Web has become so popular that it has almost replaced all the above Internet tools and slowly becoming synonymous Internet. The Web is the most popular place to be on the Internet. What is World Wide Web (WWW)? WWW is an organization of hypertext documents containing text, images, animation, sound, video and increasingly interactive program like multimedia. WWW is an easy to use interface and hundreds of thousand sites prepared by school; companies are on the web. Almost all the universities across the globe are having their presence at WWW. The web is truly worldwide. As simple mouse click can easily transport you from a server in India to Australia or America or Russia or Antarctica. The web is more than static test document. An endless variety of images, sounds, video and multimedia applications are used to present information. The WWW is called what is because sites around can be accessed and because documents seem to stretch web like through endless hyper links.

The WWW is thus the most important tool of Computer Based Information Technology. The web sites hosting a particular institution or organizations are searched and browsed through search engines and several them are available. Some 320 million web pages are currently are online. Search engines are required to wade through this vast mass of information and cull out the required information. The best way to access a web site, however, is to know its address technically known as Uniform Research Locator (URL). Once an URL is known the web site can be accessed directly. The India web is very meagre, however it is increasing at a good pace. Most of the ICAR institutions are in process of developing web sites and it is expected that by the end of this year all the ICAR National Institutes, National Research Centres, Project Directorates, State Agricultural Universities, Directorate of Extension will have their own web sites. National Institute of Agricultural. Extension Management and National Institute of Rural Development have already their websites with URL http://WWW managcari.com/and http://WWW. nird.com/. More and more extension information is expected to be on the web in very near future. The packaging and hosting of technical extension material and establishing connectivity at Krishi Vigyan Kendras, District Agricultural Officers, District Rural Development Agency, Krishi Upaj Mandis and other participating agencies has to be taken up side by side.

Computer Based Information Technology can help the extension worldwide in the following ways:

1. Facilitate interaction among research scientist, extension workers, farmers and other rural people through e-mail.
2. Providing up-to-date news and information services such as market prices and weather conditions.
3. A question and answer service among Scientists, Extension Functionaries and Farmers, where respond to queries on

specialized subjects are expected.

4. Creation and maintenance of statistical database on Agricultural and rural development parameters that can be queried on demand.

5. Providing status of various Government Programmes and details about their implementation mechanism.

6. Launching online rural development and extension journals, newsletters, latest technological information etc.

7. Hosting web sites by SAU, ICAR Institutions etc. participating in agricultural extension, putting latest packages of practices for various agro-eco regions. The institutions will also be able to get direct customer feedback for their packages.

8. By providing Internet access at district and block level Agricultural and rural development offices. This service may also be open for rural communities. This connectivity can also be used to download online publication on useful topics from anywhere in the world.

9. Opening of Cyber Cafes to enable educated rural people and extension workers at village level to have direct access to WWW for having market information etc.

10. By providing video clips to demonstrate complex procedure and audio files for rebroadcast on local radio station (FAO 1999).

11. By providing mechanism of user/beneficiary feedback for the Public Sector Schemes.

Conclusion

Computer Based Information Technology thus can be used as a complement in conjunction with existing extension and rural development and also for modernizing Agriculture in 21st century. No doubt it cannot and will eliminate all the problems of existing programmes and schemes. And in most cases Computer Based Information Technology will not even replace the traditional extension. Instead, it will both add to and subtract from today's extension methodology. It will add more interactivity. It will add speed. It will add two way communications. It will add to wider age and also more in depth messaging. It will widen the scope of extension and improve quality. It will subtract costs, reduce time. It will reduce dependency on the chain of extension system, and it will change the whole method of extension in 21st century. The continuing rapid development of telecommunications and Computer Based Information Technology is probably will be the biggest factor for change in extension one which will facilitate and reinforce other changes. There are many possibilities for the potential applications of the technology in Agricultural Extension.

Information Technology will bring new information services to rural areas which farmers, as users, will have much greater control than over current information channels. Even if every farmer does not have a computer terminal, Cyber Cafe/Cyber Extension will be readily available at local information resource centre, with computers carrying expert systems to help farmers to make decisions.

REFERENCES

FAO (1993) The Potentials of Microcomputers in Support of Agricultural Extension, Education and Training. Rome: FAO.

Goel. A.K. (2000) Agriculture Production Scenario in 21st Century. *Manage Extension Research Review,* Vol. 1, No.l, Jan-June 2000, pp-19.

Lange. Gerland. (1998). New media - An Opportunity for Developing Countries? The Global Information Society. Agriculture + Rural Development, Vol. 5, No.1, April 1998, pp. 25-28.

Sharma. V. P. (2000) Cyber Extension in the Context of Agriculture Extension in India. *Manage Extension Research Review,* Vol. I, No. I, Jan-June 2000, and pp. 24-41.

Venkataramani, G. (1999) Ushering in a New Era. The Hindu Survey of Indian Agriculture 1999. pp. 33-34.

14

AGRICULTURAL EXTENSION IN THE 21st CENTURY
Challenges and Strategies

— *R. Saravanan* and *N.S. Shivalinge Gowda*

Agriculture extension as a social innovation and a prominent force in bringing about agricultural development and socio-economic progress. In India, during the 'Green Revolution era' technological intervention lead to achieve 'foodgrain sufficiency' enhancing 50 mt in 1950-51 to 200 mt in 1997. Over the years, public extension system has been playing a crucial role in disseminating technologies and to achieve higher production. The increasing population in India, poses great threat to foodgrain requirement. The current one billion population is likely to reach 1117 million by 2010 AD. Agricultural land available and water resources have already reached the limits. In future, increasing productivity emphasizes on technological intervention by competent and accountable extension service and this situation throws certain challenges to extension system.

Needs and Challenges of Agricultural Extension

Public Extension System

Although public extension service has contributed for achieving self-sufficiency in foodgrain production, in recent past it is generally disappointing in transferring improved agricultural technologies from research to farmers in developing countries (Rogers, 1987). Indian agriculture has recorded an alarming knowledge-practice gap. India has 30,000 Agricultural Scientists generating scientific information to serve 103 million farm families. There are 127 agro-climatic zones in the country with a variety of crops and animal production system wherein there is lot of scope for adoption of improved technologies. It is estimated that about 30 per cent of the available technologies are adopted by the farmers (Hansra and Adhiguru, 1998). The commonly indicated causes for this gap are inadequate ineffective extension education, inadequate input supplies, inadequate credit support and inadequate marketing infrastructure. According to Antholt (1992), Governments also understood the limitations of public extension service attempted to very often reluctantly, the real limits of their ability to centrally manage manpower intensively and decentralized functions such as agricultural extension. Public extension is particularly vulnerable, it is too blamed, rightly are wrongly for yielding few results, imposed on farmers and run with little consideration and cost-effectiveness (Ameur, 1994).

Financial Concern

Fiscal crisis and economy wide budget cutbacks which are often associated with structural and functional adjustment programmes have forced the government to make sharp reductions in the budget allocation for public extension programmes. Financial sustainability and cost effectiveness have become the priority concerns. With the dwindling government budgets and changes in public priorities, it has been argued that several government services including extension should be 'demand driven'. Dinar (1996) has reported changes in public expenditure (reduced budget allocation) for extension as documented in several countries over the last decade. Estimates also indicated that, more than 80 per cent of public extension expenditure goes only for salaries of extension personnel.

Commercialization of Agriculture

Opportunities and challenges of agriculture in GATT with India signing the WTO, there is an urgent need to switch from subsistence agriculture to commercial agriculture that too with competitiveness to global agriculture trade and changing economic scenario. In future, commercial, specialized and capital intensive farming will demand the most accurate information of market and viable technologies. High level of investment in commercial farming requires quick and technically sound advice (Hassanullah, 1999). The farmers need to be alert with multiplying technological inflow and market intelligence at national and international level. Information support system and networking is desirable to meet the global challenges of agriculture.

Agricultural Technologies

Technologies drived from 'top down' centralized research proved inappropriate to farmers (Witcombe, 1999). Recently it has been realized that farmers knowledge should be incorporated for better results. Current public extension system transferring technologies are not economically viable, not operationally feasible, not suitable, not matching with the farmers needs and not compatible with farmers overall farming system (Hansra and Adhiguru, 1998).

Extension Clientele

Over the years the belief of 'trickle down' effect through 'contact farmers' has not taken place upto the expectations. Farmers from many developing countries have expressed serious doubts whether the Ministry of Agriculture tries to serve their interests rather than the interest of elite people or of politicians and their relatives (van den Ban and Hawkins, 1996).

Public extension policy and extension personnel never considered women cultivators are independent entities, they always treated women cultivators in rural area as a part of household or appendage to men. Agricultural technologies are often designed and disseminated without considering women cultivators.

In India most of the agricultural extension agents are men. Estimates indicated that, only 0.59 per cent of farm extension workers are women (Country Report, 1995). Men extension workers mainly concentrate on male farmers and it is not easier to communicate by male extension agent to women cultivators in rural area due to socio-cultural difficulties.

In public extension system, farmers are careless of a service, lack of interest in getting quality service (Keynen *et al.*, 1997). Reluctance of farmers towards improved farm practices due to illiteracy, prejudice against innovation; weak economic base of the farmers and poor farm resources hinders the adoption of new technologies (Saravanan, 1999a).

Public Extension Personnel

Public extension personnel are less motivated and are less trained (Ameur, 1994). Non-accountability of extension personnel, more target oriented programmes, more office work and bureaucratic nature of approach with political interference in public extension has made the system to become least effective. Public extension personnel are also facing problems such as; lack of encouragement, appreciation and recognition for good work; lack of result oriented incentives and rewards, poor chance of promotion, inadequate need based training and inadequate teaching resources.

Private Extension System

A study conducted in Bihar, Kerala, Maharashtra and Rajasthan showed that the participation of private sector in agricultural extension activities is limited to only few crops (especially horticultural crops) and select geographical regions (having high potential) (Sulaiman and Sadamate; 2000). An investigation in Tamil Nadu State indicated that the private agricultural consultancies have emerged after mid 90s. Most of these consultancies are non-registered, mostly run by a single technical person, covering small area, mainly concentrating on all aspects of horticultural crops. Further, the study indicated that 95 per cent of farmers had favourable attitude towards privatization (Saravanan, 1999b), similar results reported in Haveri district of Karnataka where 76.59 per cent of farmers had favourable attitude towards privatization (Hanchinal *et al.*, 2000).

Strategies to meet the Challenges in Agricultural Extension Service

- Encouraging farmer participatory technology generation and dissemination through participatory techniques like PRA, RRA, PLA, PTD and critical incidence technique should be employed.
- More emphasis on incorporation of farmers indigenous knowledge and their experiment in technology generation and dissemination.
- Generating location specific, need-based technology and efforts to popularize the same.
- Adequate inservice training facilities for extension personnel to make competent and update their knowledge.
- Commercialization of certain specific demand-driven technologies in public extension to promote self-sufficiency of extension organizations.
- Partial privatization of extension service in a phased manner.
- Identifying targeted clientele group who are eager to try new technology and commercial in their venture:
- Providing more partnership rights to NGOs in technology transfer.
- Selection of women cultivators as contact farmers and organizing extension activities exclusively for women folk.
- Recruitment of more women extension personnel.
- Formation of women cultivators' groups for easy dissemination

of technologies and providing incentives for progressive women farmer.

- Exclusive training programmes for women cultivators.
- More emphasis on market information management in agricultural extension.
- Application of advances in information technology for agricultural technology transfer and for providing market information.
- Establishing in-built mechanism for periodical evaluation of extension programmes.

Conclusion

Agricultural extension in the 21st century demands structural and functional changes through appropriate strategies such as farmers participatory technology generation and dissemination, more concentration on women cultivators, phased manner of privatization of extension service and application of information technology to disseminate innovations. This makes extension system more efficient and effective to meet the current challenges and future needs of the farming community.

REFERENCES

Ameur, C., 1994. Agricultural Extension : A step beyond the next step. *World Bank Technical Paper*, No: 247, The World Bank, Washington DC., USA.

Antholt, C.H., 1992. Relevancy, responsiveness and cost effectiveness: Issues for agriculture extension in the 21st century. *Journal of Extension Systems*. 8: 3 7-44.

Country Report, 1995. Fourth world conference on women, Beijing 1995; Country Report, Dept. of Women and Child Dsevelopment, Ministry of HRD, GOI, New Delhi.

Dinar, A., 1996. Extension Commercialisation: How much to charge for Extension Services. *American Journal of Agricultural Economics*, 78(1): 1-12.

Hanchinal, S.N., Sundaraswamy, B.and Ansari, M.R., 2000. Attitudes and preferences of farmers towards privatization of extension service. *Abstracts Volume of National Seminar on Private Extension: Approaches and Challenges in New Millennium*. July 28-29. 2000: MANAGE; Hyderabad.

Hansra, B. S. and Adhiguru, P., 1998. Agriculture transfer of technology approaches since Independence in India: *Journal of Extension Education*, 9(4).

Hassanullah; 1999: Agricultural extension service of the 21st century – needs and challenges. Presented in the *Regional Symposium of Agricultural Extension Education*. Mymensingh, 18-21, April, 1999. Bangladesh.

Keynan, G., Manuel Olin and Ariel Dinar; 1997; Co-financed public extension in Nicaragua. *The World Bank Research Observer*. 12(2): 225-47.

Saravanan, R. 1999b. A study on privatization of agricultural extension service. M.Sc. (Ag. Extension) thesis (unpublished). Department of Agriculture Extension. UAS; Bangalore:

Saravanan, R. 1999. Problems and future of public extension service. *Seminar Report*, UAS; Bangalore:

Sulaiman. V. R. and Sadamate, V.V., 2000. Scope of privatizing farm extension; *Annual Report* (1999-2000), NACP. ICAR. New Delhi.

van den Ban, A.W. and Hawkins, 1996. *Agricultural Extension*, Blackwell Science Ltd. Pub., Oxford; pp. 256-258:

Witcombe, R.J., 1999. Do farmer participatory methods apply more to high potential areas than to marginal one's? *Outlook on Agriculture*. Z8 (1): 43-49.

15

PARTICIPATORY VIDEO FOR SOCIAL CHANGE

—*H. Philip* and *Sriram*

Gandhiji was so effective in this communication because he was not a professional communicator. Although he wrote every day like a journalist, the message came from the heart and needs of the people. He used the medium of salt for communication and his message become meaningful to the poorest of the poor.

The worldwide growth of the electronic mass media in the 1960 and 1980 produced the so-called information explosion. However, these electronic media, largely government controlled, have essentially followed a one-way information flow from government agencies to the rural population with little or no concern for the voice of the villages. Besides, there has been obvious urban-bias in content, language and treatment by the mass media.

There is a great difference between the roles and capabilities of the person tackling the real problem at the grassroots and the professional communicator or media technician. A leader of a vegetable vendors can make tapes which directly benefit her constituency and which are effective channels of participation, empowerment and awareness-building play a vital role in society, they cannot have these participatory characteristics.

It is essential to know the important distinction between the goals of communication i.e. 'tackling' the real problem and the media tools which serve those goals. For many people it is almost revolutionary to argue in favour of putting 'sophisticated' technology in the service of poor people in developing countries. This challenges many of our assumptions about media and technology.

Placing video in the hands of the people will be useful to achieve a goal. Professor E.V. Chitnis, former Director, Satellite Application Center, Indian Space Resource Organisation, reported that more than ten years his collegues and himself have trained groups of literacy teachers, women organisations, family planning workers and others to use video as a tool in their work. Their programmes about a village that is energy self-sufficient, a community health centre, child labour and how to form a cooperative are incorporated into their local organising and development work. These video produces have uncovered communication processes that reach of his or her voice. They have pioneered participatory and empowering methods consonant with their culture and context.

Some of these video teams make programmes without using editing equipment and many have only one camera. Their programmes meet local, not international needs and some play a role in a process rather than standing on their own as 'finished' tapes. While their work may lack fancy special effects and technical polish, it excels in profound impact and strong, honest content.

Participatory Video for Social Change

Professional media maker's work is done when they file the story or when they hand over the finished edited tape. In contrast, the work is largely beginning for the participatory video maker. He or she will be involved in facilitating play backs of the tape, in building on the insight, motivation and understanding the tape creates, and in continuing working toward the long-term goals that the tape is serving.

Sara Stuart, President, Martha Stuart Communication, New York, explained about a case of participatory video efforts often begin with workers' education classes. They generally involve one week of training and discussion in which the goal is to raise awareness among a particular group of self employed women workers of their common difficulties and encourages the women to organise.

Understanding the strength and power of collective action comes slowly to the grass-roots women who participate in worker's education classes. For many it is completely a new idea; they have taken exploitation for granted all their lives. They video taped several of their demonstrations one by vegetable vendors and another by garment worker. The recordings show hundreds of poor women marching through the streets of Ahmedabad and chanting their demands. Although, they are made very simple, without editing, these tapes are perhaps the most powerful and most often used video. They raise spirits, inspire confidence and solidarity, and communicate effectively the importance of collective action.

Sara Stuart took this tape of the garment workers' procession to a women group who do *chikan* embroidery. They are the worst paid women group and conservative Muslims. She organised training with them and talked about organising and coming out of their homes and not wearing *purdah*. On the last day she showed this tape and they were so exited and jumped up to plan out the route for their own procession. In reality, they were nowhere near the stage where they could take out a procession but this enthusiasm is helping them to get organised. When women actually see that people like them have succeeded through organising it makes a really big difference.

Video is well suited to horizontal exchange of experience

Video is lightweight and portable, requires no processing and is immediately available, it can easily serve as a vehicle for exchange at the grassroots. This is particularly valuable to participatory approaches as ideas or techniques can be introduced for discussion and consideration by villagers in a fairly neutral manner having to advocate or push the group to take action. Video makes it easier to grasp new ideas and it is even simpler if the viewer feels something in common with the person on the tape.

For example, when video was introduced to a group of literacy teachers as a part of literacy project first they were suspicious about the equipment. They did not want to work. But when a programme was played about a women's co-operative movement and they saw it was their reality, they had confidence. They saw that it was not for their publicity but rather in educating them. Since the tapes were in their language they could easily understand everything.

Sara Stuart also explained another case. In 1984, when they invited the women to the training sessions in a village, the husbands would not let their wives to come. During the next year, all the villages saw the video programmes about the training and they saw the women were learning about farming and nutrition. After this exposure there was no problem with their husbands.

When a video programme in success story mode will attract more. For example when a video programme highlighting the advantages of the drum seeder explained by a progressive farmer of Pollachi taluk of Coimbatore district of Tamil Nadu was screened to the farmers of another village received a good impact. The programme not only increases the knowledge of the farmers but also made them to adopt. Now the entire village and other neighbouring villages also using the drum seeder for paddy planting.

Good Communicator can make an Effective Tape

Video puts illiterate viewers as well as illiterate producers on a par with their literate counterparts. This levelling or equalising aspect can transform relationships and support a high level of participation. The following points to be considered to become a good communicator to make an effective tape.

1. Knowledge on the subject he is going to be video taped
2. Involvement in field production
3. Little knowledge on video equipment
4. Able to highlight the subject to the viewers point of view

5. Able to establish human relation among the participants of the programme
6. Able to establish good relationship with the viewers
7. Fluent in local language
8. Familiarity with the local dialects

It is possible to use video in ways that are very empowering

Every can participate in and benefit from the use of video and all can gain strength through their involvement. Operating video equipment is empowering especially for grassroots producers. Appearing on a video, seeing yourself and telling your own story via video can be tremendously reinforcing and motivating. Finally people at the grassroots are at the very bottom of society's information hierarchy. They need to communicate their needs and concerns to people at all levels and to receive many kinds of information but particularly from others whose experience is relevant to their situation. This is a prerequisite to their full participation in society.

I think of what I have seen in Brazil and with the Inuit of Northern Quebec. In both areas, organising begins with identity and culture. The Inuit are making tapes that strengthen and preserve their traditions. They feel that communicating is central to their survival of their way of life. Although materialism in filtering into their society, they place the greatest importance on their communication.

On the other hand, in Brazil, a society inundated by media, popular or community video is extremely successful. These programmes contain a great deal of music and entertainment, reminding us that development is not just serious business; it is also fun. Even in the *favelas* the people are media savvy and they value media that convey their own experience and reality. In these very different parts of the world with completely different media environments, participatory video is proving a potent tool in strengthening local culture and building self and community system.

Participatory Videos are simple to make, Expensive and Reach Smaller Audiences

Participatory video need not be of the highest quality. In many cases, the immediate feedback is the most important use of the recording. Simpler and faster production techniques such as in-camera editing fit the objectives of people who are tackling the real problem. Still, it would be a mistake to generalise that all grassroots video is low quality. Some is very beautiful and many teams support their activist work by providing production services for profit.

Professional media makers are generally interested in producing programmes which reach the largest audiences and have the highest technical quality. Although participatory video producers produce programmes of very high quality and occasionally they may reach mass audiences, this is not the goal of their work and they do not compromise substance or approach to reach mass audiences.

Any film that aims for an audience of a million people must be highly generalised in both topic and language. This is viable only if your audience shares certain minimal economic level and class formation.

If you want to direct your film to a peasant audience, you immediately have to acknowledge the differences... You immediately have to contend with particularity. I believe that if you want to address issues in depth, you need to make concrete films for specific groups. The economy of the new technologies encourage this.

Because video is re-usable and considerably less expensive than film, it can take the narrow audience approach much further. Video SEWA produced a tape which achieved its goal and had a very positive impact by reaching an audience of one. In this case video was a channel of negotiation between the vegetable vendors in a way he could never have in a face-to-face confrontation. The vendors spoke in a way they would never have spoken to representatives of the municipality.

From the standpoint of change, the most important

characteristic of video is its potential to have a profound, positive and making a impact. In my opinion this distinguishes it from most mass, non-participatory media which have the marvellous ability to reach millions, to raise issues, to create awareness on topics and to disseminate information with great efficiency. But, there is no way to alter the passivity of the mass media receiver nor the central structures which control these media. In contrast, participatory video can lead to action and assist change.

16

SUSTAINABLE PUBLIC EXTENSION SERVICE

Issues and Strategies

— *A. Shaik Alauddin*

The majority of poor people in developing countries live in rural areas, rely on agriculture for their employment and spend a high proportion of their income on food (UNDP, 1998). In general, agricultural extension services are supposed to contribute to livelihood improvements for all groups of farmers (better-off, resource-poor, women) as well as to increase the overall agricultural production of a country including the provision of foreign exchange from export of agricultural products. However, most of the farmer households, in particular the resource poor households, are not reached by any frontline extension workers. Public agricultural extension has for decades been heavily criticised for its many shortcomings and failures.

At national level there is a need for developing extension policies and strategies which promote effective and sustainable extension services for farmers. Economic sustainability is of vital importance and every country should develop an extension strategy that fits within its financial means. Underfunded extension staff not only become frustrated by not being able to carry out their duties effectively, but also rapidly lose their credibility with the farmer (IFAD, 1996). Structural adjustment programmes, changes in the role of the State, decreases in public spending, reductions in the number of extension agents have contributed to the need for realism and rethinking when it comes to economic sustainability of public extension.

Conflicting Objectives?

What is the purpose of agricultural extension? Are the objectives clear and shared among the different actors on the extension arena? Agricultural extension services are supposed to fulfil many aims, from reducing rural poverty and improved livelihoods for rural households to increasing the overall production and contributing to foreign exchange earnings from export.

At government level agricultural production is seen as a source of foreign exchange and government revenue and as a strategic tool that can be used as means of control, a political weapon and an instrument of social welfare. Individuals on the other hand, are more concerned about achieving stable or increasing food production, cash income, energy forest production, leisure time and decreasing production costs, debts and uncertainty in general (Nkowani, McGregor and Dent, 1995).

Is the question production contra people or how to combine the two? Do we have to choose between increasing the overall production and improving the livelihoods of resource-poor rural households? This basic assumption or philosophy is critical because it will inevitably influence the extension approach and, consequently, also the structures appropriate for its facilitation (Duvel, 1995).

Hence, the mandate or objectives for extension services must be clearly defined in order for extension to achieve its goals and to be evaluated accordingly. Besides, evaluation of public extension services reveal inefficiency and lack of impact; extension agents without a clear sense of what they are expected to accomplish, poorly motivated workers and management, top-down approaches, no accountability to farmers, inappropriate messages, lack of supervision, lack of linkage with research etcetera. If we add on the context in which extension operates, such as lack of political commitment; decreases in public spending; changing role of the State, privatisation; market failure, lack of incentives to foster agricultural production and development; differential access to land, labour and capital as well as opportunities; externally imposed change programmes; and unrealistic assumptions, we get a better understanding of why public extension services perform badly.

The Target Group Question

The underlying philosophy and explicit objectives also discourse the next issue of target groups. Who should be served by which extension service? Should all groups of men and women farmers be served, from large-scale commercial farmers to peasant subsistence farmers? Is it possible to serve such a diverse target? Who should prioritise? The traditional approach to extension has been to rely on the so-called progressive farmers, meaning better-off men farmers, who are generally easiest to reach, less averse to risk and have access to sufficient resources of land, labour, physical and human capital. (Nkowani, McGregor and Dent, 1995). It is therefore logical that in the place of its present role as a delivery mechanism for the predetermined messages the extension system assumes its established responsibility as a non-formal educational service, with more explicit development goals to meet the demands of target groups.

It is anticipated that gradually the farm sector will develop into two district phases under the influence of the market-oriented new economic policy. A segment of the farm sector, consisting of venture some and resource rich farmer, a group of resource poor farmers under an umbrella of farmers cooperatives and a group of farmers around urban centres, involved in commercial production of flowers, fruits and vegetable will move towards rapid commercialization of farming, having the domestic as well as exports markets in viewers. The production effects of farmers here will have to meet required standard and strict quality control. Perforce, the individuals and groups of farmers will necessarily require precise technical support and hence the need for specialised extension service. The other segment constitute a major proposition of farming population viz., the small scale often largely subsistence farmers, who could be served through a general extension service, like the present day public extension service.

Public or private extension is not necessarily an either/or choice, but perhaps both. The question is what might be most effective where and for whom. Private extension services will serve different groups of farmers than public extension. The main clients of private funded extension service will likely be market-oriented medium and large-scale farmers.

Issues in Public Extension Service

The present day public extension system taken new technologies developed at research stations and passes them in a top-down fashion to farmers. They have largely accrued to the larger farming with more resources, who with all the factors of production at their command have been able to adopt the research recommendations with little risk. Expert opinion has converged, indicating that the present extension system has not performed as it was expected. Notwithstanding its research linkages, its reliance on the contact farmers and its preoccupation with the regular, training and visit activities, its achievements have remained far less than adequate. This system is not proved to be successful in making adequate use of the available technology. One possible reason is that it did not devote the required time and effort with the responding farmers, since all the faith was put to contact farmers. Moreover, this system was not equipped to tap the creativity and potentiality of innovative farmers found in every community.

Experiences from World Bank Projects

Many of the more successful extension Projects financed by World Bank, involving group formation have been drawn on existing traditional groups. A good example is provided by Indonesia, which has been introducing the Training and Visit (T&V) system, and has been able to build on a number of such traditional groups. Rural people in Indonesia have lived and worked for centuries with strong communal groups or cooperatives such as *subak* (farmers' associations formed for use of irrigation water), *gotong royong* (farmer's self-help association), and *mapulus* (farmers' mutual assistance association). These have a clear membership, and high loyalty to the leader, and for introducing T&V extension, these farmer groups have become the focus for guidance and technology transfer.

Historically, they had been rather hierarchical with a tendency to operate in a top-down fashion, and so when the T&V system was introduced the traditional leader often became the contact farmer. Now, however, they have moved to identifying subgroups in adjacent field areas and matching up farmers with different resources levels to have more representative contact farmers. They discuss and agree their seasonal extension programme, decide on technology appropriate to their situation, and monitor feedback from questions posed at the regular visit of the extension worker. In this way they have become much participatory. The village receives special training in maintaining group dynamics, and the local administration gives active encouragement.

Another example is from a pilot project in the Midlands of Zimbabwe that has been running for the last two years. Here again there is a strong tradition of work associations for sharing agricultural labour, and more recently of savings groups that have been especially strong among women. Here, farmer groups organized for extension purposes are normally sub-divided when numbers exceed thirty, to keep practical demonstrations effective and retain the groups' cohesiveness. A key feature is that the final stage of dissemination of improved technology is done by farmer representatives themselves, two of whom are selected to attend each training session fortnightly and to report back to the rest of the group. This is a tenet of the T&V system but rarely is it institutionalized and done so effectively. The chosen contact farmers rotate amongst group members depending on their individual attributes related to the topic under discussion. This enables several members of the group to be both trainee and trainer, and by going together it reinforces their mutual knowledge of the lesson being discussed. The fortnightly training sessions, which other farmers may attend as well as group leaders, are conducted on members' plots, and group leaders rotate their training of fellow group members around different member farms. Slogans in the vernacular and songs about the lessons have all helped to motivate keen participation by all members, especially the women. Whereas less than 10 per cent of farmers were in groups before the pilot scheme started two years ago, groups covered about 70 per cent by mid-1985.

Issues and Strategies for Group Approach in Public Extension

- The main issue in group formation is that the group has to recognize the need and the benefits to be obtained from forming a group, and in maintaining it. This means care has to be taken in forming the first group and in demonstrating to others the value of having them. Group formation, which is politically or administratively, imposed from above rarely workers, and the groups will be short-lived if members do not derive benefit from them. There has to be relevant technology that group farmers can adopt to their advantage to ensure active participation, and this has to be revised and enhanced as the group develops. Relevant interventions are thus needed for initially starting groups, that will strengthen as they realize the benefits of a new relationship and improved interaction with research and extension staff, as well as starting to have more of a say in their own destiny which governments have to listen to.
- Likewise, farmers need to be stratified according to their resources, so that technologies extended are relevant to their conditions. Such groups can be sub-groups of a larger group, their nature varying according to the social structure and the cohesiveness of the society. The Zimbabwe example demonstrated the need to split up groups when numbers exceeded thirty for effective extension communication, but the size of the group will vary according to traditional social factors, such as the size of family or kinship group.
- Members must take part in leadership selection, and rotating leadership as used in the Zimbabwe groups has much to

commend it, especially when associated with their acknowledged varying technical expertise in different farm enterprises under discussion. It is suggested that the people specially trained for the task should fulfil this role. So that they can diagnose and analyse with farmers their problems and present options (not just one recommendation) for their solution.

- The public extension service should not be focussed towards any seasonal crops alone but it should deal with a avoid range of technologies including agriculture, horticulture, animal husbandry, sericulture, forestry, fisheries with careful and meticulous planning. So that the technologies put forward by the public extension system can be effectively filled into a field extension work and overlapping is avoided in transmitting the technology.

Conclusion

At national level, the extension services are impacted by the global trends of privatization, market liberalisation and decreases in public spending. Public extension strategies need to involve groups not only to ensure more farmers are reached at lower cost, but more importantly to provide viable local institutions that can help farmers to be most self-reliant, and to sustain development investments. Successful group development has a major role to play in as well as reducing costs to government, which is less well equipped in any event to play such a role permanently. Sound technology, well adapted to local conditions, is a necessary prerequisite to build on, requiring better trained extension staff, better attuned to farmers' needs and prepared to work as equals with farmers other than to farmers. For we have to remember that all research and extension activities are only a means to an end: increased productivity on the farm, and the well-being of the farmers. The farmer is central to all these activities. And to disregard his or her vital input is to guarantee that must research and extension activity will be irrelevant and not a cost-effective use of scarce budgetary resources.

REFERENCES

Chamber, R. A. Pacey and L. Thrupp (Eds) (1989). *Farmer First: Farmer Innovation and Agricultural Development*, London: Intermediate Technology Publications.

Chambers. R. (1994). *Beyond Farmer First*, London: : Intermediate Technology Publications.

Duvel, G.H. (1995). In search of International Linkages for Participatory Extension in Agricultural and Rural Development, *European Journal of Agricultural Education and Extension.*

IFAD (1996). IFAD's evolving experience with extension support in Eastern and Southern Africa. Paper presented at the second informal consultation on International support to agricultural extension systems in Africa, Rome: IFAD, October 8-9.

Nkowani, K., McGregor and B. Dent (1995). The stagnation of small holder agriculture in the Northern region of Zambia: Problems. conflicts and production systems. *Outlook on Agriculture*. 25(3). 103-109.

UNDP (1998) *Human Development Report*. New York, UNDP.

17

TECHNOLOGY AND AGRICULTURAL DEVELOPMENT
Scaling New Heights

— *Seema* and *R. Annamalai*

In the hoary days of its public sector, India developed strong capabilities in the design, planning and execution of irrigation projects, big dams, petrochemical plants and refineries etc. In the new era of globalisation, we must ensure that this expertise is developed further and that we remain a strong technology power. It is because technology has become the "Prime Mover", "Push Factor" of progress. Especially in case of agriculture, to win in the world economy, the prime mover namely the technology is the key determinant and will continue to remain a dominating factor of development in future (Naik, 1999).

Scientific Discovery, Production Advance and Prosperity Improvement

A few basic steps are needed if we want to convert the scientific breakthrough now taking place in most crops, farms, animals and in inland and coastal aquaculture into a production advance and a production advance into improved prosperity for all sections of the rural community. First, all groups must accept the concept of productivity. For this purpose, minimum productivity targets will have to be fixed and a farmer who does not achieve the target continuously for a few years without valid reasons should stand every chance of losing his land. Minimum targets such as 3 tonnes per hectare per year from two crops on irrigated land and one tonne per heactare per year in areas with over 1000 mm rainfall are neither ambitious nor unrealistic if proper institutional arrangements are made for supporting farmers. Appropriate Agricultural Productivity Acts by our State Governments could provide the social compulsion for cooperative efforts in areas like soil and moisture conservation and pest control. The second need is to match the obligations of farmers under Agricultural Productivity Regulations with corresponding obligations on the part of State Governments. For this purpose, the Gram Sabhas or Panchayats may have to be restructured in such a manner that every member of the panchayat assumes specific responsibility to organise the social support necessary for the effective adoption of a technological innovation. Unless there is a link between those who move society and those who move science and technology, it will be difficult to achieve the ends we desire.

Research Development System

With the shift in emphasis of agricultural production from 'sustenance' to 'commercial enterprise' research and developmental requirements also undergo changes in approach. Because of the pervasive weakness the research and development system the "technology-push" is constrained. If the research and development system is to meet genuine needs in industrial and agricultural production:

- research priorities must be correlated with the actual technological issues confronting the production system,
- The performance of the entire agricultural system, its institutions and its management must be measured in terms of the techno-economic impact of its programmes and projects on individual users and on a particular sector, and

- Resource budgeting for the research and development system must be to relate to the economic pay-offs at the end of the technology delivery process.

The linkage between the research and development activities is most effective where they are carried out on the initiatives of both public and private enterprises in a coordinated manner.

Technology and Changing Needs

- Improved scientific technologies, even when sound by scientific standards, are of limited value if they are not adopted due to their inappropriateness to suit the ágro-climatic and socio-economic milieu in which the farmers operate. Non-adoption of such technologies by the clientele group has been ascribed to:

- inappropriateness of the technology to specific situations,
- inadequacy of support services and inputs to adopt the technology,
- socio-economic and soico-cultural constraints,
- non-availability of required technical support to implement the technologies, and
- managerial constraints and ineffectiveness.

In developing countries which operate their research and extension systems with the avowed objectives of increasing food production and meeting the challenges of increased demands for food, fibre and fuel, quick development of location specific technology and their wide dissemination and adoption are very critical. It demands the holistic approach that defines the problem in precise terms and the output expectations in quantitative terms. The approach should register systematically the benefits arising from a group of technolgies, the demands that they will create, and the risks attendant with it; all these are to be considered together holistically.

Meeting the Challenge through Technological Approach

From the foregoing, it is obvious that unless the latest tools of science and technology for the sustainable and equitable use of the natural endowments of a country are applied, poverty and hunger will persist. The development and transfer of technologies that are ecologically, economically and socially sound and desirable must receive the over riding priority in any country's developmental agenda. Every country will have to develop a technology policy based on optimum blend of three approaches:

- Preserve indigenous technology and improve it further, in the context of quality and efficiency of output and marketing arrangements.
- Shifts to the frontiers of tehnology in fields such as micro electronics, computer applications, remote sensing and satellite imagery, biotechnology, genetic engineering and communication.
- Upgrade traditional technologies and improve their market competitiveness without losing soical, ecological and economic advantages by integrating traditional and frontier technologies.

To sum up, what should be the basic characteristics of improved technologies for the future? There are at least five basic requirements: higher productivity, higher profitability, greater acceptability, greater stability and greater sustainability. These can be achieved only if we are able to integrate the needs indicated in the symphonic agriculture matrix into agricultural strategies, shown in Table 17.1.

New Research Agenda Vital

Even with effective policies, responsive institutions and a proactive outreach programme to provide the poor with access to financial services, agricultural renewal will not occur if the technology of agriculture does not change. It is here that the impact of agricultural research is decisive.

Table 17.1 : Symphonic Agriculture Matrix

Needs	Technology	Services	Government Policies
Ecology	Conservation and enrichment of environmental assets	Associations for sustainable development	Agro-ecological rehabilitation
	Farmer participation in location-specific technology development	–	Long-term commitment
Economics	Cost reduction with-out yield reduction	Timely and adequate supplies of inputs	Input and output pricing policies
		Management tools	Home and internatio-nal trade
Equity	Small farmers	Knowledge, skill, input transfer	Political will and action for ensuring livelihood, security
	Women	Diversification of on-farm and off-farm employment	–

The challenge facing global agriculture in the next century are arguably greater than at any previous time. A new research agenda needs to be implemented for the new millennium, one that is innovative, appropriate and effective. The task involves a double shift in the research paradigm.

The first shift is the contextualisation of crop research. This is well known, but has not yet been achieved: that is the integration of the crop specific research, which has been so successful in the past, into a broader, more holistic vision that brings in the concept of sustainability and looks to achieving results through increasing the productivity and profitability of complex farming systems at the small holder level. It involves recognizing the synergies between the management of livestock, agro-forestry, food and cash crops, and acquaculture – all on a hectare or so. The second shift is to harness the genetic revolution. We must utilise the most cutting edge work associated with genetic mapping, molecular markets and bio-technology to accelerate the breeding process and achieve the promise of all that science can do for the poor and the environment.

Conclusion

Technological change in agriculture can stimulate growth in income and employment in many sectors of the economy. As national economics get integrated into the world economy, technology has become a tradable product par excellence. Countries which have realised this are reaping the benefits of it by investing substantial resources in research and development, so as to remain at the frontiers of technology. India at present invests about 0.46 per cent of its agricultural GDP in research and development. The role of harnessing science including biotechnology, information technology, enlightened human resource and strengthening of national and international partnerships are indeed critical. Therefore, there must be an increased national commitment for appropriate agricultural policies to ensure the required economic growth. Lack of foresight today will obviously prove costly in the future.

REFERENCES

Naik, K. 1999. Post Green Revolution Agriculture: Micro level Perspective, International Development Paper, p. 368.

National Research Council. 1992. *Alternative Agriculture*, Washington National Academy Press.

Swaminathan, M.S. 1996. *Science and Integrated Rural Development*. Concept Publishing Company, p. 354.

Swindle, L.D. 1990. Sustainable Agricultural Production: Final Report of the CGIAR Committee, CGIAR Document No. 90/18, The Hague.

18

EFFECTIVENESS OF INSTRUCTOR CONTROLLED INTERACTIVE VIDEO PRESENTATION IN TRANSFER OF TECHNOLOGY

— *C. Selvaraj* and *H. Philip*

Education Commission (1964-65) and All India Conference on Agricultural Education (1969) strongly recommended that appropriate method should be used to stimulate teaching-learning process. Most of audio-visuals fail to make any interaction in the teaching-learning process. Interactive Video (IV) fulfils the needs for the interaction in the communication process. The interactive video being costly and individualised in structure. It needs skill to handle. The instructor can replace the computer and make the learner group watch and record the iteraction by responding to the questions asked by the instructor, intermittently. Feedback could be given to the learners for their response through the video controlled by the instructor. Hence, a study was conducted to find out the effectiveness of Instructor Controlled Interactive Video (ICIV) among farmers at different age and education groups.

METHODOLOGY

The study was conducted in the Perambalur devision of Perambalur Co-operative Sugar Mills Ltd., Eraiyur, Perambalur district of

Tamil Nadu. Four villages were selected at random. Video programme on "IPM on sugarçane" was prepared with the help of professionals of Tamil Nadu Agricultural University, Coimbatore. Four exposures of Instructor Controlled Interactive Video (ICIV) on "IPM on sugarcane" were conducted in selected four villages at the rate of one exposure/village. Each experimental group consisted of 30 respondents representing two age levels of upto 35 years and above 35 years and two educational levels of upto 8th standard and above 8th standard. In total 120 sugarcane growers were selected at random as respondents.

FINDINGS AND DISCUSSION

To find out the knowledge gain and symbolic adoption through ICIV among different age-education groups, the data were collected by using well structured and pre-tested questionnaire, processed and presented in the Tables 18.1 to 18.8.

I. Effectiveness of Video among Age-Education Groups in terms of Knowledge Gain

Effectiveness of video among age-education groups in terms of knowledge gain is presented in Table 18.1.

Table 18.1 : Mean Knowledge Gain among Age-Education Groups through Video

Age-education groups	Mean knowledge score		Mean knowledge gain score	Percentage
	Before exposure	After exposure		
A_1E_1 (G_1)	2.02	3.60	1.58	78.21
A_2E_1 (G_2)	2.69	3.68	0.99	36.80
A_1E_2 (G_3)	1.74	4.98	3.24	186.42
A_2E_2 (G_4)	2.44	4.71	2.77	93.03

From Table 18.1 it could be seen that the group G_3 had gained maximum knowledge through video among respondents compared to other groups. The percentage of knowledge gain through video was accounted to 186.42 per cent. This was followed by groups G_4, G_1 and G_2 and accounted to 93.03 per cent, 78.21 per cent and 36.80 per cent respectively. It could also be observed that G_3 and G_4 had gained more knowledge when compared to the other groups. Higher education status of the groups may be the reason for this increased knowledge gain. Among all the groups, G_3 had gained more knowledge (186.42%) than others. The present finding derived confirmation evidence from the finding of Stephens (1980), Abraham (1981) and Philip (1995). From this it could be concluded that young respendents with high level of education gained more knowledge through video.

Effectiveness of Interaction among Age-Education Groups in terms of Knowledge Gain

Effectiveness of interaction among age-education groups in terms of knowledge gain is presented in Table 18.2.

Table 18.2 : Mean knowledge gain among age-education groups through interaction

Age-education groups	Mean knowledge score		Mean knowledge gain score	Per-centage
	Before exposure	After exposure		
A_1E_1 (G_1)	3.60	5.17	1.57	77.72
A_2E_1 (G_2)	3.68	4.77	1.09	40.81
A_1E_2 (G_3)	4.98	7.28	2.30	132.33
A_1E_2 (G_4)	4.61	6.20	1.49	61.06

The group G_3 had the highest mean knowledge gain through interaction of 2.3 (132.33%). This was followed by the group G_1 (1.56) and accounted to 72.72 per cent.

This was also followed by the mean knowledge gain through interaction with regard to groups G_4 (1.49) and G_2 (1.09) and this accounted to 61.06 per cent and 40.81 per cent respectively.

This might be due to the fact that the young aged respondents with high level of educational status had more knowledge gain through interaction compared to old aged respondents with low level of educational status.

Effectiveness of ICIV Among Age-Education Groups in terms of Knowledge Gain

Effectiveness of ICIV among age-education groups in terms of knowledge gain is presented in Table 18.3.

Table 18.3 : Mean Knowledge Gain among Age-Education Groups through Instructor Controlled Interactive Video

Age-education groups	Mean knowledge score		Mean knowledge gain score	Per-centage
	Before exposure	After exposure		
A_1E_1 (G_1)	2.02	5.17	3.15	155.44
A_2E_1 (G_2)	2.69	4.77	2.08	77.69
A_1E_2 (G_3)	1.74	7.28	5.54	318.76
A_2E_2 (G_4)	2.44	6.20	3.76	154.09

It could be observed that the G_3 and G_4 had high level of mean knowledge gain of 5.54 (318.76%) and 3.78 (154.09%) respectively. This was followed by G_1 (3.14) and G_2 (2.09) which were lower educational groups and accounted to 155.44 per cent and 77.69 per cent respectively.

From this it could be very clearly observed that high education status was responsible for high level of knowledge gain through ICIV, irrespective of age groups. From this table also, it could be observed that the role of age and educational status in increasing knowledge gain.

Effectiveness of ICIV among Age-Education Groups in terms of Symbolic Adoption

Effectiveness of ICIV among age-education groups in terms of symbolic adoption was presented in Table 18.4.

Table 18.4 : Mean Symbolic Adoption among Age-Education Groups

Age-education groups	Mean symbolic adoption	Percentage
A_1E_1 (G_1)	2.33	69.90
A_2E_1 (G_2)	2.48	74.40
A_1E_2 (G_3)	2.52	75.60
A_2E_2 (G_4)	2.51	75.30

It could be seen that the viewers of upto 35 years of age with higher education (A_1E_1) had the highest symbolic adoption followed by the viewers of above 35 years of age with higher education (A_1E_2). This was accounted to 2.52 (75.60%) and 2.51 (75.30%) respectively. This was followed by the groups A_2E_1 (74.40%) and A_1E_1 (69.90%) respectively.

There is not much variation among the different age-education groups. This means that ICIV was very effective in symbolic adoption of technologies among all age-education groups without much variation.

II. Effectiveness of Video among Age Groups and Education Groups in terms of Knowledge Gain

Effectiveness of video among age groups and education groups in terms of knowledge gain is presented in Table 18.5.

Table 18.5 : Mean Knowledge Gain among Age Groups and Education Groups through Video

Age-education groups	Mean knowledge score		Mean knowledge gain score	Percentage
	Before exposure	After exposure		
A_1	1.88	4.29	2.41	128.19
A_2	2.57	4.20	1.63	63.42
E_1	2.34	3.64	1.30	54.45
E_2	2.09	4.84	2.75	131.80

From Table 18.5 it could be seen that the age group of upto 35 years (A_1) gained more knowledge (128.19%) compared to the other age group of above 35 years (63.42%). The reason might be due to the viewer's capacity to observe and understand the subjects very clearly. In case of educational groups, the viewers with higher education (E_2) have gained more knowledge (131.80%) compared to the education group of upto eight standard (54.45%). This is well known fact that high educational level will influence the viewer's understanding capacity and made them to know technologies better. This present finding is in conformity with that of Hansra and Chopra (1984) Selvaraj (1990) and Philip (1995).

Effectiveness of Interaction among Age Groups and Education Groups interms of Knowledge Gain

Knowledge gain through interaction among age groups and education groups are presented in Table 18.6.

Table 18.6 : Mean Knowledge Gain among Age Groups and Education Groups through Interaction

Age-education groups	Mean knowledge score		Mean knowledge gain score	Per-centage
	Before exposure	After exposure		
A_1	4.29	6.13	1.84	98.13
A_2	4.20	5.49	1.29	56.35
E_1	3.64	4.97	1.33	56.31
E_2	4.84	6.65	1.81	86.60

From Table 18.6 it could be observed that viewers of higher education (E_2) had gained more knowledge (86.60%) than that of other education group (56.31%). Higher educational qualification of the groups might be the reason for higher knowledge gain. In case of age groups, the respondents of age upto 35 years gained more knowledge (98.13%) than those were of above 35 years (56.35%) of age . It is the fact old aged viewers were lacking with the participation ability when compared to young aged viewers and probably this would be the reason for loss of the knowledge gained by the old aged viewers.

Effectiveness of ICIV among Age Groups and Education Groups in terms of Knowledges Gain

The results of age groups and education groups with regard to the knowledge gain through ICIV are presented in Table 18.7.

The Table 18.7 reveals that the education group E_2 had higher knowledge gain (218.80%) than the education E_1 group (110.80%). Among age groups, A_1 had shown higher knowledge gain (226.32%) than the A_2 group (114.20%).

Table 18.7 : Mean Knowledge Gain among Age Groups and Education Groups through Instructor Controlled Interactive Video

Age-education groups	Mean knowledge score		Mean knowledge gain score	Per-centage
	Before exposure	After exposure		
A_1	1.88	6.13	4.25	226.32
A_2	2.57	5.50	2.93	114.20
E_1	2.35	4.97	2.61	110.80
E_2	2.09	6.66	4.57	218.80

Higher educational status and young age might be the reason for them to get higher knowledge gain through ICIV. It can be attributed to their high intellectual capacity, more enthusiastic participation and also their eagerness towards the new technologies on sugarcane cultivation.

Effectiveness of ICIV among Age Groups and Education Groups in terrms of Symbolic Adoption

The results on the effectiveness of ICIV among age groups and education groups on symbolic adoption are presented in Table 18.8.

From the Table 18.8, it could be easily observed that the mean symbolic adoption was almost same due to the effect of ICIV among all age groups (A_1 and A_2) and education groups (E_1 and E_2). This finding is derived support the findings of Chandrakandan (1982) and Selvaraj (1990).

Table 18.8 : Mean Symbolic Adoption among Age Groups and Education Groups Instructor Controlled Interactive Video

Age-education groups	Mean symbolic adoption	Percentage
A_1	2.43	72.75
A_2	2.50	74.85
E_1	2.40	72.15
E_2	2.52	75.45

III. Factors associated with the Effectiveness of ICIV among Sugarcane Growers

The association of the characteristics of respondents towards knowledge gain video, interaction and ICIV and also symbolic adoption through ICIV.

It could be observed that age, farming, experience, and annual income had exhibited negative association with knowledge gain through video. The variables education and farm size had positive association with knowledge gain through video, whereas occupation had no association with knowledge gain through video.

It could also be inferred that age, farming experience and annual income had exhibited negative association with knowledge gain through interaction. The variables education and farm size has positive association with knowledge gain through interaction whereas occupation had not associated with knowledge gain through interaction.

It could be observed that age, farming, experience and annual income had exhibited negative association with knowledge gain and symbolic adoption through ICIV. The variables education and farm size had positive associated with knowledge gain and symbolic adoption through ICIV. Whereas occupation had no association with knowledge gain and symbolic adoption through ICIV.

Higher education could have made them to analyse the technology and gained more knowledge. This is in conformity with the findings of Selvanayagam (1980) and Philip (1995). Higher farm size should have facilitated the viewers to search for the new technology and thus resulted in high knowledge gain. This is in conformity with the findings of Reddy (1971), Singh (1971) and Sridhar (1983).

The negative and significant association of age might be due to the fact that youngsters were very attentive to know the new things and gained more knowledge. This is in conformity with the findings of Meenakshisundaram (1990) and Jeyasubramanian (1996). Less farming experience and low annual income might have facilitated the viewers to learn the appropriate cost effective technology early and thus resulted in high knowledge gain. This finding is on par with the finding of Meenakshisundaram.

Conclusion

The study conclusively demonstrated the fact that the farmers with age upto 35 years and educational status of above 8th standard A_1E_2 had gained more knowledge and symbolic adoption when exposed to ICIV followed by video and interaction. It is also concluded from the study that the respondents with the age up to 35 years (A_1) and also above 8th standard of education (E_2) were found to have high level of knowledge gain and symbolic adoption were exposed to ICIV followed by video and interaction. Except occupation all the other five variables exhibited a significant association with knowledge gain through video, interaction and ICIV and also symbolic adoption through ICIV. Education and farm size had positive association whereas age, farming experience and annual income had negative association with knowledge gain through video, interaction and ICIV and also symbolic adoption through ICIV. So ICIV could be used effectively among young and highly educated farmers to impart knowledge on new technologies and induce symbolic adoption.

REFERENCES

Abraham, S. 1981. Farm Telecast - An Ex Post Facto cum Experimental Study. Unpub. M.Sc. (Ag.) Thesis; TNAU, Coimbatore.

Balasubramanian, N. and M. Enigo Charles, 1994. Instructor Controlled

Interactive Video - An Appropriate Technology for Agricultural Extension in the Proceedings of the International Workshop on Alternative and Cost Effective Extension Approaches for Sustainable Agriculture: Methodological Issues, Organised by FAO and TNAU, Coimbatore.

Chandrakandan, K., 1982. Effectiveness of Farm Broadcast on Listeners Affective, Cognitive and Psychomotor Behaviours. Unpub. Ph.D. Thesis, TNAU, Coimbatore.

Hansra, B.S and R.K. Chopra., 1984. Knowledge Gain and Retention of Socio-personal and Psychological Stigma of Televiewers. *J. Res., Punjab Agri. Univ.*, 23 (4):

Jayasubramanian, B., 1996. Impact of Distance Education Programme of TNAU through Correspondence Course: A Diagnostic Analysis. Unpub. M.Sc. (Ag.) Thesis, TNAU, Coimbatore.

Meenakshisundaram, K.S., 1990. Television Viewing Behaviour of Farm Women. Unpub. M.Sc.(Ag.) Thesis, TNAU, Coimbatore.

Philip, H., 1995. 2D and 3D Visuals for Effective Video Programme Production - An Experimental Study. Unpub. Ph.D. Thesis, TNAU, Coimbatore.

Reddy, S.V., 1971. Leadership in Relation to the Interpersonal Communication Behaviour. Unpub. M.Sc.(Ag.) Thesis, IARI, New Delhi.

Selvaraj, G.,s 1990. Effectiveness of Video Teaching on Farmers Affective, Cognitive and Psychomotor Behaviour. Unpub. Ph.D. Thesis, TNAU, Coimbatore.

Singh, R., 1971 A Comparative Study of Adoption of HYV Programme by the Farmers of TV and Non-TV Villages. Unpub. M.SC.(Ag.) Thesis, IARI, New Delhi.

Sridhar, V.R., 1983. Farm Telecast - An Analysis of Impact and the Viewers Preference. Unpub. M.Sc. (Ag.) Thesis, TNAU, Coimbatore.

Stephens, Nancy Jane., 1980. Influence of Age on Learning from Television Advertisements. USA: The University of Texas at Austin, Ph.D. Dissertation. *Dissertation Abstracts International*, Vol.41, No. 04, Oct. 1980, p. 1268 A.

19

PRIVATISING EXTENSION SERVICES FOR MODERN AGRICULTURE

A Tool for Promoting Commercial Agriculture in Indian Farming

— *G. Selvaraj* and *Ravikumar Theodore*

The new millennium has dawn with challenging targets, opportunity, threats and problems which has raised the unequivocal question whether the public extension system will be able to deliver the goods. The increasing awareness and need for commercialisation, export agriculture, food processing and value addition, organic farming, Agri-business, sustainability etc., has placed much pressure on the public sector extension, to operate at a very high standard now-a-days. But with the general resource crunch fiscal deficit, and budgetary limitation sustaining the huge extension machinery by the government is proving to be a difficult task and is becoming a burden on the exchequer. Notwithstanding with this problem with the aim of protecting the interest of the farmers who are mostly small farmers, the government continues to fund and maintains the vast extension network and infrastructure. So there is an alternative to meet the requirements of the poor farmers as well as to reduce the burden of the government. At this juncture it is important to bring to light certain successful extension services provided by the private firms and organization that have been widely accepted by the people as success stories.

History

The evolution of private agricultural extension around the world was initiated during 1980's. In the developed Industrial countries which exists as a model for the extension service delivery elsewhere, the declaiming relative importance of agriculture for economic growth and increasing use of externally purchased inputs have changed the public funded extension services and lead to questioning the means of extension delivery system by the government agencies.

In New Zealand the privatisation was gained momentum during 1993 (according to Bloom, 1993). The privatisation services were introduced as an external force.

The main concentration was focussed on cost recovery of technology transfer. According to Rovera and Gustafson, 1991, the more commercial attitude of the system has created tension between extension worker and their clients which ultimately fragmented knowledge and information system by regular information flow.

The models as quoted by Prost and Rolling (1992), the Netherlands government has tried the model DLV acts as a foundation for a partnership extension service between farmer organisation and the Dutch government. The information knowledge centres were act as a central office which are all with the private organisation for the in and outflow of the information. The government forms had a share of farmers to the tune of 5 per cent. Due to this the country like Netherlands with dense population and small farms is next to U.S. in terms of agricultural export.

In Indian context, the private sugar factories plays a successful image to the farming community that they could change the knowledge, attitude and skill of the farmers through various selected extension mean and methods. The farmers in the sugar belt area were quite convinced due to the proven technology transmission by the private sugar industries. Since, majority of the farmers were not in a position to take up the recommended input by the sugar factories. The sugar factories they themselves arrange the total inputs right from the sugarcane setts, herbicides, pesticides, fertilizers including harvest and transport charges. Since the private extension service created confidence among the minds of the farmer and they were quite definite about the income they started cultivating sugarcane on a large scale making the country to feel as the second largest producer of sugar in the world chasing Brazil to occupy the first position. The farmers were not expected to pay initially for the technical support given by the sugar industries. The private companies has taught related skill in sugarcane production technology not only to the cane growers but also to 3.5 lakh skilled and unskilled workers also. They were in favour of scrupulously following the technology advocated by the sugar industries. This is an ideal example how a private extension service can safeguard the interest of the farmer as well as the interest of the country.

Sugarcane as a Value Added Product

Sugarcane is a multiproduct crop and therefore it has lot of avenues for use of its by-products and co-products like co-generation, paper, newsprint and boards from bagasse, chemical and alcohol from molasses and animal feed from the ligna-cellulosic residues will help to boost the production as many large and medium sized industries can be established using sugarcane as raw material. This will again act as an alternative for the decline of International sugar price apart from the various byproducts mentioned above rural based cottage industries producing jaggery as an important component, particularly in view of their contribution to rural economy and its nutritive value.

Another right example for a successful privatisation of extension is the tea industries. For example, the role of united planters association of South India, the small and the large growers joined together as a joint venture to do both research and extension for its members. This organisation concentrated not only on increasing the yield but quality production also. Due to the introduction of WTO as a global regulatory mechanism which is said to dominate in the years to come. In order to survive in the new millennium there is no other ways and means except to take the competition on quality. So, any industry should have plan for the quality and safety standards that are likely to be more demanding in future. The concept of total quality management as propounded by ISO 9000 has gained much importance by the tea industries. The tea industries were also started on hazard analysis critical control point which provides the hazards that are likely to occur in different stages of manufacturing and marketing.

Conclusion

The success of the above cases clearly indicates that private extension need not be constructed as competition to the Government extension services rather than it should be taken as a complementary efforts as being adopted in China with the private extension. The government extension service can join hands to exchange their own expertise in order to meet the supply and demand of the farming community. The trend will facilitate the free flow of information in rural areas and make the agriculture more productive and profitable. When the educated youth feels that farming is a profitable avocation definitely. There will be an active participation of youth in the agricultural sector too as in the case of industries. This will again provide some job opportunities to the rural youth and again reduce the migration from rural to urban areas. Due to the introduction of Farmers market by the Government of Tamil Nadu provides an active platform to accelerate rural marketing for various consumer products.

20

FUTURE PROSPECTS OF AGRICULTURAL EXTENSION

— *Seema* and *R. Annamalai*

Technology adoption by agricultural producers is an essential pre-requisite for economic prosperity for a country. The adoption has been influenced by technological information passed from the research system to the extension system and finally targetting the needy. It is universally felt that extension system should respond to the needs and requirements of the society. In the context of meeting the holistic needs of increasing agricultural production yet do so in a sustainable manner, agricultural extension has a crucial role to play. Reforms in extension management envisage greater focus on optimization of available resources, management of inputs and agro-services for higher efficiency, decentralization of processes and raising the overall economic efficiency of agriculture.

Future Policy Reforms

Reforms in the system envisage an extension service more broad based and holistic content and scope, thus beyond agricultural technology transfer. Reforms in agricultural extension already initiated and proposed to be undertaken on wider scale are discussed below :

Promotion of Demand-driven and Farmer Accountable Extension

Under the T&V system the technology dissemination regime was more supply driven. Research and extension agenda's were pre-set based on technologies for high yielding varieties of wheat and rice. An important reason why research and extension organisations have not focussed on farmer's problem is due to the lack of an effective feedback system. The vast majority of small and marginal farmers in India, especially women, lack an effective voice in influencing, research and extension priorities. Under the new policy agenda a demand drivers extension system will be created by providing farmers with access to linkage mechanisms through which they can articulate their problems and needs. A key factor in improving these feedback systems is to organize farmers into functional groups such as SHG's, farmer interest groups (FIG's), commodity associations (CA's) and/or other types of farmer organisation (FO's). These FO's can provide an effective channel for both the dissemination of technology to large numbers of small and marginal farmers, and they produce an effective feedback channel to research and extension.

Multi-agency Extension Service

For many years agricultural extension was considered the monopoly of the public sector. However, with the wide range of demands of agricultural technology in the changing scenario there is growing recognition that public extension by itself cannot meet the specific needs of various regions and different classes of farmers. The new extension region recognizes the role of a multi-agency dispensation comprised of different strengths. Policy environment will promote private and community driven extension to operate competitively in roles that complement, supplement, work in partnership and even substitute for public extension. The three arms of the agricultural extension network are:

Public Extension Service

- State Government line departments operated extension (Department of Agriculture, Horticulture, Livestock Development)
- State agriculture based extension (Directorate of Extension, KVK, Krishi Gyan Kendras)
- ICAR extension (Zonal Research Station, Agri. Technology Information Centre, Institute Village Linkage programme)

Private Extension Service

- Community Based Organisation (Farmer's Organization, Farmer's Cooperatives, SHG)
- Para extension workers (contact farmers, like farmers, Mitra Kisans, Mahila Mitra Kisans)
- Input suppliers/dealers (pesticides, seeds, nutrients, farm implements)
- Corporate sector (commercial crops–tobacco, tea, coffee, seeds, farm implements)

Mass Media and Information Technology

- Print media–vernacular press
- Radio, TV, private cable channels
- Electronic connectivity through computers, NICNET, INTERNET etc.
- Public and private information shops.

Promotion of Farmer Participatory Approach

There is a need of more farmer's participatory approach in working out the system description, problem diagnosis, search for appropriate technology, designing the process of implementation, monitoring and evaluation and feedback. The extension agent is no longer seen as the expert who has all the useful information and technical solutions; the indigenous technical knowledge of farmer's knowledge and their ingenuity, individually and collectively, are recognised as a major source; solution to local problems are to be developed in partnership between the extension agent and farmers. Extension workers therefore used new skills of negotiations, conflict resolutions and mobilizing and nurturing community organizations.

Strategic Research and Extension Plans (SREPs) through Participatory Rural Appraisal (PRA)

In the process of creating a more bottom-up extension system PRA procedures would be introduced across all system levels (district, block, mandal and village) and across each participating line departments (DOA, DOH and DAH) and research institution (ZRS and KVK) within the district. On the basis of PRA, SREPs would be prepared for the district. The district SREP must be grounded at the block or mandal level, where extension programmes can be fine-tuned to the needs of farmers and more effective implemented.

Strengthening Research–Extension–Farmer Linkages

Close interaction between farmers, extensionists and production systems researchers in diagonising problems together and working out location-specific recommendations emphasizing participation education rather than prescription and joint actions in the field. There is a need to strengthen research-extension-farmer linkage not only at the State and SAU levels but also at the district level not only between Department of Agriculture and SAUs but between department of horticulture, department of animal husbandry, fodder, agro-forestry, soil and water conservation, silvipasture as well as on-farm land and water management in a farming system approach. The research extension interface at all levels from district to national level is needed.

Developing Professionalism in Cost Effective Manner

Training institutes/centres may focus on developing core competency, other services may be out-sources or contracted-feedback from participants must be used to evaluate performance of faculty.

Involving Farmers in setting Extension Agendas

Farmers representation as major stakeholders should be ensured in all decision-making bodies of public and private extension service. Farmer should be involved in planning and implementation of extension programme through formal institutional mechanism like Farmer's Advisory Committee etc.

To hasten the transfer of technology, extension has to be reoriented, redirected and transformed into a more viable force, for this it is essential to understand the problems encountered in disseminating technologies and search for the appropriate solution to make the process more effective and viable. In this context some of the major problems encountered by the extension workers and suggestions for the same are given below:

Problems encountered	Suggestions given
• Lack of conviction in the new technology on the part of extension worker and the farmer.	• Need based technology generation.
• Most difficult attribute of empowerment is participation.	• Need to organise the village community participation will have their demand on extending services like roads, drinking water, housing etc.
• Agricultural Research Institutes concentrate there efforts on research and technology generation and extension agencies concentrate their efforts on technology dissemination with negligible attention to technology integration.	• Proper linkage and effort is needed between both agricultural research and extension agencies.

(Contd.)

Problems encountered	Suggestions given
• Lack of research and education in area of importance	• Necessity to identify specialised areas like– Biotechnology, Agri-business,Trade and export etc.
• In absence of clear directions, research or extension personnel concentrate their efforts on those activities, which they consider important–training is not emphasized linkage activities.	• Additional effort needed for coordinating and building expertise.

Conclusion

Extension mechanism will have to be driven by farmers need, be location-specific and address diversification demands. There is room for both the public and private sectors in the development of a demand based feedback driven system technologies required to address total farming systems are knowledge intensive. Hence, the time has come now for agricultural extension to cope with the changing scenario with its new strategy and approach to reach farmers not only with basket of technological options but also with information of new market opportunities on gain, more profit and sustainability of income.

REFERENCES

Ameur, C. 1994. Agricultural Extension: A Step Beyond the Next Step, World Bank Technical Paper, Washington.

Das, P. 1996. Changing Scenario of Agricultural Economy and Future Thrusts in Extension, *Journal of Extension Education*, 7(2&3): pp. 1390-1393.

Maalouf, W.D., T.E. Contato and R. Adhikarya, 1991. Extension Coverage and Resource Problems: The Need for Public Private Cooperation, *Agrl. Extension*, Amsterdam, Elsevier.

Policy Framework for Agricultural Extension. 2000. Krishi Anusandhan Bhavan, ICAR, New Delhi.

Singh,Y.P. and Babu Ramesh,1997. Utilization of Extension Research in India, *Journal of Extension Education*, 8(3): pp. 1725-1730.

van den Ban, A.W.1997.Changing Ideas on Agricultural Extension– A Global Perspectives, *Journal of Extension Education*, 8(2) pp. 1638-1650.

21

INFORMATION FLOW AND DEVELOPMENT CHALLENGE

— *Seema* and *R. Annamalai*

The present economic liberalization, as a product of globalization, has been typified by unprecedented expansion of private capital, free markets, advanced communication and production technology into every corner of the globe, undoubtfully change the world agricultural scenario. This situation calls for the shift towards commercial and export oriented agriculture, demands information based approach to agricultural communication, which aids in decision-making, collection of accurate, relevant information and their timely distribution to the potential users. Thus, IT are indispensable catalysts of agricultural development in the twenty-first century where sustainability and profitability of agriculture leads to a complex situation.

Agricultural Communication Facing Challenges

The total communication system including the mass media and extension services had failed to reach the rural poor and equip them with skills necessary for making the best use of new opportunity (Yadava, 1974). The reasons were the absence of sound communication policies, ineffective coordination of communication efforts and frequent information loses at every level of communication system (IIMC, 1979). Towards the twenty-first century, the economic liberalization and the consequent changes in the global agricultural scenario have characteristically structure Indian agriculture as a diversified and commercialised venture which in turn contribute significantly towards country's economic growth. In this context, the farmer must be competent enough in collective decision-making in order to harness the benefits of emerging technologies. Of course, the farmers accumulated experience can strengthen his overall competence, but a great deal of it comes through his ability to obtain and utilise informations emitted from different sources. In this situation, the speed and ease of information access may enable the farmer in an early decision-making. But too often, the public extension system fails to provide an information link to the rural poor and those who need it, due to lack of knowledge and skills of ways in which it can be achieved (Ban, 1993). Apart from the farmer, the other agencies like agro-processing industries, traders, merchants, cooperatives, agricultural policy makers, national planning bodies and international agencies involved in developmental work also demand information for decision-making. Thus, to provide timely and accurate information to these various agencies, the information technologies can create a strong infrastructure, which is seldom possible through other means.

Technologies for Agricultural Development

The communication revolution, as witnessed by the prolific growth information technologies, has truly revolutionalized the communication scenario. These wonder technologies offer a great scope for speedy and easy access to information along with higher accuracy. With their abilities of interaction, demassification and asynchronisation, they induced a new thought of development. These technologies include:

Microcomputers : The advanced, sophisticated digital microcomputer is capable of performing multiple operations like management analysis, input calculations, crop modelling creation and storage of databases, the computer terminals or microcomputers with modems linked to the telecommunication network can provide access to database anywhere in the world. For example, the agricultural researchers may gain access to the FAO databases in Rome (Hudson, 1990).

Advanced Satellite System : Indian National Satellite System is multi-agency, multi-purpose operational satellite system for domestic long distance telecommunications, nationwide direct satellite TV broadcasting to augment community TV receivers in rural and remote areas, and nationwide radio and TV programme distribution for re-broadcasting through terrestrial transmitters, meteorological earth observation and data relay.

Blue Tooth Technology – the universal interface : It is a universal radio interface that enables portable electronic devices– simultaneously and without wires – to contact to and communicate with up to seven other units. Applications of this technology are truly unlimited.

Windows CE – shared and synchronised information: Windows CE is an open, scalable windows platform for a broad range of communications, entertainment and mobile computing devices. The standard based windows CE platform is an operating system that allows now-PC consumer devices to communicate with each other. It also allows access to Internet to send or to receive E-mails or to browse the web.

Teletext : This electronic magazine can be used to relay a variety of information to a restricted audience. In addition, some specialized information may also be delivered to a segment of society.

Videotex : The interactive two-way communication service is capable of catering an individuals specific need. This consumer oriented service supports a variety of information based services and interact transactions in the marketing of agricultural commodities.

Problems in Use of Information Technology

The underlying problems which cause shortcomings in use of information technologies can be grouped into three main types, namely, operational problems, contextual problems and strategic problems (Bhardwaj *et al.*,1995).

Operational Problems

(a) *Technical constraints:* Non-availability of appropriate and latest technologies.

(b) *Economic constraints:* Non-existence of reliable background information about IT and inadequate capital resources to invest on them.

(c) *Weak basic infrastructure:* Non-availability of and intermittent failure of electricity and inadequate telecommunication infrastructure in rural areas.

(d) *Deficiency of skilled human resources:* Inadequate technical and operational expertise in order to manage information technology.

(e) *Lack of maintenance of infrastructure:* Breakdown of latest and imported equipments may create inconveniences due to non-availability of spare parts in domestic market.

Contextual Problems

(a) *General conceptual inadequacy about the use of IT:* Lack of clarity about the potential of IT among various developmental officials and the general public as well as lack of management awareness among top officials about their applications in long-term planning.

(b) *Misfit of IT into Indian organizational and socio-cultural environment:* Since, most of the new technologies are developed in industrialised nations to cater their needs, the introduction of them into Indian conditions may create the problem of misfit with the administrative/managerial and socio-cultural environment.

(c) *Existing lower literacy rate among rural adults :* Can hamper the introduction of language biased IT's in rural areas.

Strategic Problems

(a) *Absence of comprehensive policy support :* To channelise the use of IT's in agriculture and prevailing import restrictions are also responsible for stagnation in penetration of these technologies into the development stream.

(b) Weakness of domestic research and development support to support indigenous production of technologies, increase out independence on advanced countries for acquiring technologies, at a higher cost.

(c) Dicotomous application of IT's in rural areas, virtually widens the gap between information rich and information poor.

Conclusion

The shift towards commercial and export oriented agriculture, demands information based approach to agricultural communication. No doubt, the emerging information technologies offer a great scope for collection and dissemination of information. The recent developments in Indian IT scenario depicts on positive backdrop to apply these technologies for catalysing development, whose investment is anticipated to increase from Rs. 1,377 crores in current years to Rs. 2,079 crores in 2000-2001. Thus IT are indispensable catalyst of even agricultural development if planned and applied carefully, can revolutionize agricultural communication in this new millennium.

REFERENCES

Bhardwaj, N.B. Kumar and A. Dimri 1995. New Information Technologies for Farm Development, *Communicator*, Vol. 30 (4): 330-36

Cummings, R.M. 1981.Minimum Information Systems. *Agricultural Information Development Bulletin*, Vol. 3 (3): 2-10.

Hudson, H. 1990. Information Technology: Challenges for Development. *Agricultural Information Development Bulletin*, Vol. 12 (4): 2-4.

Karnik, K. 1996. Emerging Communication Scenario. *Mainstream*, Vol. 34 (38): 9-14.

Various issues of *The Hindu* (2000).

Yadava, J.S. 1974. Communication Strategy and the Challenges of Rural Development. *Communicator*,Vol.14 (2): 4-10.

22

OFFICELESS EXTENSION SYSTEM FOR FARMER DEVELOPMENT

— *S. Mothilal Nehru* and *N.K. Jayachithra*

Kerala Horticulture Development Programme (KHDP)

A joint venture of European Union (EU) and Government of Kerala (GoK) was launched in the year 1993, with the objective to improve the overall situation of commercial fruit and vegetable growers of Kerala by increasing and stabilising their income. The emphasis is on increase in production and productivity, reduction in cost of production and improving the marketing system. The functional unit of the organisation is Self Help Group (SHG), comprising 15-20 farmers, who voluntarily join together on "neighbourhood" principle. Around 10-15 SHGs join to form a Field Çentre (FC), catering to the needs of 200-300 SHG member farmers. As on date there are 33,306 SHG member farmers of 1538 SHGs in six Project Areas/districts.

The Agricultural Extension system prevailing in India is such that in each State, the Director of Agriculture, supported by a team of District Level Principal Agricultural Officers initiates the planning process. Within a district, at the Block level, Assistant Directors work in collaboration with the Agricultural Officers at Panchayat level. In this organisational pattern, the Agricultural schemes/projects are planned at the higher ups and implementation takes place in Panchayats. The loophole of this system is that there is no provision for the participation of farmers in the planning process. A change in this pattern of oraganisation was brought about by the People's Plan Campaign in Kerala in the late 1990's. This system envisages the consideration for aspirations and needs of local people and their locally available resources, while working out the Panchayat level plans. The micro level plans of Panchayats are integrated at Block level to bring out the Block level plan and such Block level plans in turn are integrated at District level which forms the basis for the final district level plans. The panchayats / local bodies are also authorised to implement their plan depending upon the local resources available.

Table 22.1 : District-wise Vegetable and Banana Farmers in KHDP

District	No. of Panchayats	Banana		Vegetable		Total	
		No. of SHGs	No. of farmer	No. of SHGs	No. of farmer	No. of SHGs	No. of farmer
Trivandrum	29	129.	2676	177	3417	306	6093
Kottayam	31	29	567	264	6521	293	7088
Ernakulam	32	131	3267	119	2576	250	5843
Thrissur	29	127	2281	130	2310	257	4591
Palakkad	20	61	1243	165	3610	226	4853
Malappuram	23	36	872	130	2991	166	3863
Kozhikode*	05	16	361	24	614	40	975
Total	152	529	11267	1009	22039	1538	33306

Source : MIS Report as on 03.10.2000, KHDP

* During 2000-01, KHDP has initiated replicating its activities in the new Project Area i.e., Kozhikode.

Thus the Peoples Plan follow the principle of "By the People and for the People". The KHDP model is a step still closer to the micro level of organising local people and their resources at group level.

Extension Approach – KHDP Model

The KHDP model is an improvement of the Training and Visit (T&V) Extension system which was introduced by the World Bank about 25 years ago. This model is unique in the sense that at the Micro level (site/panchayat) for about 200-300 cultivating farmers of 10-15 SHGs, there is only a single officer who has no office building. The contact point between the officer and farmers may be a crop field/farmers house/field centre; where the officer holds meeting, conducts training and provides guidance to the SHG members. The Officeless system is needed because field offcers should spend atleast 80 per cent of their time in the field and it is more so in case of vegetables and fruits since they are short duration and perishable crops which are susceptible to pests and diseases. This officer is called the Assistant Manager-Field Centre (AM-FC). She/he is responsible for implementing the FC based plan related to Transfer of Technology, Training, Group Marketing and Credit delivery. Apart from these activities, campaigns, field level diagnostic visits, crop demonstrations, study tours, SHG meetings etc are also organised by the AMs. As well as these officers introduce novel micro level concepts such as group level common fund. They arrange centralised input centres and bulking point for the local produce. Through the process of empowerment these activities are later taken up by the SHG level farmers. The "Officeless" approach, which is not only conducive for extension staff to spend all their time in the field, but also reduces the need for additional support staff.

There will be such 20-30 AMs for different FCs in a Project Area/District where KHDP operates. These AMs and their FC level activities are coordinated, monitored and reported at the District/ Project Area level by a Manager – Project Area(M-PA). The M-PA is also supported by a team of Project Area Resource Group (PARG) members. There will be one AM-Production & Technology, one AM-Training, one AM-Credit and one or two AM-Marketing in the PARG team. The Manager(s)-Project Area of the different Districts/Project Areas report to the Director of Project Planning & Implementation (DPPI) of the Programme Directorate. Thus the KHDP Directorate gets the picture of the entire field level operations under the Programme in different Project Areas. On the other hand, the Horticulture Resource Centre (HRC), under the guidance of Director-HRC, with the supporting AMs of different units at

Headquarters provide the resource support such as planning and designing and preparing formats and documents for field level implementation. There is a balanced proportion of 1:4:20 among top, middle and junior managerial staff in KHDP. Around 10 top, 40 middle and 200 junior managerial staff form the backbone for the harmonious development of the Resource Support and Field Implementation wings of this organisation.

Highlights of the Model

Planning and Reporting System of AMs at Project Area Level

At the end of every financial year, the FC level AMs prepare their field level plans, for the next year in consultation with the MFs of SHGs and the M-PA. Based on this plan the officer initiates activities in the forthcoming year. The action plans of all the AMs–FC will together be integrated to arrive at the Project Area level action plan (otherwise called the M-PA's action plan). The action plans of PARG members are prepared in consultation with the respective units at the Directorate and respective Project Area levels.

Transaction in the Project Area Monthly Review Meeting

The AMs-FC of each Project Area directly report to the M-PA only once in a month. During this meeting only, they share their performance in the field and submit the report of the field level activities (Field Report) undertaken by them in the previous fortnight. On the same day they will plan for the next fortnight and handover a copy of the next fortnight plan to the M-PA. In this meeting itself, they have to discuss the FC level problems encompassing all dimensions and find out amicable solutions for the same, in consultation with the M-PA and if needed, with the PARG members of the respective disciplines such as Training, Marketing, Credit and Production & Technology. In extreme situations it will be taken up by the top level management. The formats like fortnightly plan, field report, farmer database, credit plans, training related formats, KHDP newsletter/booklets, campaign materials and inputs like seeds and cash advances for field level activities are to be collected as well as to be settled on the same day. The circulars/internal notes of the Administration and Finance Component with regard to the leave application, attendance certificate, salary disbursal, cash advances, field claims and any other financial claims/remittance are conveyed to the field personnel in this meeting. In a month, a field officer has to prepare 1-2 page reports about their personal claims, 1-2 page reports (in prescribed formats) about their performance and has to plan for the year or half a year or a particular quarter of a year or for a month. This means that no new activities are taken up all of a sudden.

The most visible of impact of this system are :

- The field officers are in touch with the reality and are comfortable with farmers and confident about their work.
- Farmers feel the refreshing change because the field officer is available at their place i.e. in the field.
- This is a more personal and informal set-up

The system is new in that the same field officer covers all important areas of cultivation i.e., problem, solving (Participatory Technology Development – PTD, technology transfer, training, credit, marketing etc. While achieving these, the Master Farmers are getting empowered so that the system becomes more sustainable.

Project Review Meeting

At the end of every month, there is a Project Review Meeting at Headquarter level, which is presided over by the Programme Director, attended by Director- PPI, Director Horticulture Resource Centre (D-HRC) and the M-PAs representing the respective Project Areas. The meeting starts with presentation by M-PAs on implementation issues and they are sorted out. In this meeting each M-PA will present the plan and achievement of his Project Area for the previous month, which will be a consolidated report of activities of all AMs-FC and AM-PARG coming under him. This is the platform at which the Programme Directorate is able to monitor the field level implementation of activities as well as to give guidance and instruction to the respective M-PAs. This also provides an opportunity for the programme to identify the shortfalls/ drawbacks if any, and put forward suggestions to improve/smodify the strategy in field level issues of concern.

Management Information System (MIS)

The MIS component of the programme at the Headquarters, collects the planning and reporting formats of all the components and document them in computers. The fortinightly plan of an AM-FC, when entered in the computer, the MIS can provide the information on the contact point and activity of the particular AM in a particular FCs on a specified date. Similarly, the MIS maintains the Farmer Database, SHG database, reports of area and production of vegetables and banana, Training, Marketing, Credit, Participatory Technology Development (PTD) and Pest and Disease Surveillance status reports. These MIS reports act as important monitoring tools for the Programme and also make the Officeless Extension Approach a viable one.

The Role of Field Level Extension Personnel

KHDP officials in field act only as facilitators; provide only necessary technical and managerial inputs and guidance to Master Farmers of SHGs and SHG members. The objective is to equip the Master Farmers to take up the lead role in planning and implementing SHG level activities, thus enabling SHG member farmers to sustain their activities on their own accord when one SHG gets stabilised and reach a Self Help stage. KHDP does not give any subsidy or favour or interfere/involve directly in credit management or trading activities.

Conclusion

In nutshell, the plan and implementation of KHDP activities at FC level with the active participation of SHG level Master Farmers is safe in the hands of a sincere and industrious officer (AM-FC). As a recognition of the KHDP model, European Union (EU) has extended the Project for two more years to consolidate the activities as well as to replicate the model in other potential areas of Kerala. This officeless extension system has been proved to be successful in facilitating field level activities in an effective way and thereby empowering the SHG members which is unique in Indian Agricultural Extension.

REFERENCES

Bellard, Stuwart (2000). *Visit Report*, Report submitted to KHDP, pp. 4-7.

Seventh Work Plan April 2000 to March 2001. (2000). Programme Directorate, KHDP. Cochin. pp. 18-74.

23

INFORMATION TECHNOLOGY
Vision for the New Millennium

— *Beena C. Panicker* and *M.R. Choudhary*

A new revolution is sweeping the globe – information technology (IT). It is a vehicle for future development, opportunities, challenges and competition that enables information to be collected and used in the history of civilization, no work of science has had so comprehensive an impact on human development as IT. Undoubtedly, IT has been the greatest changing agent of this century and promises to play this role even more dramatically in the coming days of this millennium.

No aspect of human life remains untouched by the impact of IT and agriculture is no exception. A crucial requirement for success of development efforts is access to accurate and timely information. This crucial nature of information makes the information technology (IT) revolution important to agriculture and rural development. Modern information and communication technologies including the Internet when applied to conditions in rural areas can help improve communication, increase participation and disseminate information and share knowledge and skills. It is being said that "Cyber Extension" would be the major form of technological dissemination in the near future. The constantly changing world poses tremendous challenge and opportunities for a developing country like India. For India the rise of IT is an opportunity to overcome historical disabilities and once again become master of one's own national destiny.

This chapter is an attempt to throw some light on how information technology can play a major role in the rural development as well as to put together certain Projects where application of information technology have made difference.

Technologies and their Role in Rural Development and Agriculture

- *Compact Disc Read only Memory (CD-ROM :* is a storage medium which together with a computer offers rapid access to a large volume of information. Some of the agricultural databases on CD-ROM are AGRI (FAO), CAB Abstracts (CABI), AGRICOLA (US Department of Agriculture), TROPAG & RURAL. (Royal Tropical Institute).
- *Radio and Television :* Can reach rural audiences with specially tailored messages in an attractive and cost efficient format.
- *Decision Support System :* are Computer programmes that use knowledge, facts and reasoning techniques to solve problems and help the user make timely planning, management and analysis decisions. Programmes have been developed for a number of agricultural applications. With the help of this one can determine how much fertilizer to use, how often and how much to irrigate crops, how much pesticide to use, expected value of harvest and the best marketing or storage strategy for crops.
- *Geographic Information Systems (GIS) :* helps organize information about regions and facilitates analysis of relationships between different variables. Application includes land-use analysis: site selection, physical analysis and environmental analysis. It was found to be a cost effective way of collating and analyzing land resource data for small watersheds.
- *Interactive multimedia : integrates text:* video audio, graphics and animation permits students/trainees to learn interactively using real situations, at a time, pace and location suitable to them. It was found an effective training tool for water

management Engineers in India.

- *Communication and Information :* sharing opportunities offered by electronic communication particularly through the Internet or information super highways are tremendous. Internet gives access to a vast global information resource and support bottom-up articulation of development needs and participation and thus help in reducing the isolation of rural communities.

Some of the Projects where in application of Information technology have made differences are:

- *Warana Wired Village Project :* covering 75 villages in Maharashtra the existing cooperative structure has been used with State of the art infrastructure to allow Internet access to cooperative societies. The aim is to provide information to villagers by establishing networked booths in the villages.
- *The Information Village Project :* implemented by the M.S. Swaminathan Research Foundation is aimed at bringing the benefits of modern information and communication technologies to the poor and assetless families in village in Pondicherry. The village information shops established under this project provide information relating to health, credit, input price and availability, transport, market information, meteorological information, information far pest surveillance and agronomic practices and data an entitlements to rural families.
- *National Diary Development Board :* IT based machines are being used at Milk Collection Centres, and in cooperatives to measure butterfat content of milk, test the quality of milk and promptly make payment to the farmers. It has reduced time for payments from ten days to less than five minutes and instilled confidence in farmers in the cooperative set-up. All these factors have helped milk markets to expand.
- A CMC Pilot Project has installed a Computerized Universal Postal system and a Centralized Accounting and Reporting System in three Post Offices in Andhra Pradesh. The

technology is designed for rural environments. The system handle multifunction within a Postal Office, reduces errors and waiting time, and provides transparent transactions.

Andhra Pradesh is the first State in India to assign a statewide computerization programme that will be used in rural areas at the mandal level. There are 1,124 mandals in the State. The first software applications is the issue of certificates pertaining to land holdings, caste, nativity and income across a common counter without the current delay of fifteen to twenty days.

Thus IT has become focus area of the country's overall development and prosperity, aiming to give the country a status to emerge as a superpower in the world. Our Prime Minister Shri Atal Behari Vajpayee's vision that IT is India's tomorrow is obviously an inspiration for healthy competition in world economic and social environment.

REFERENCES

Harnessing IT, Indian Scenario, April 1998, *Extension Digest*, Vol. 1, No.7, pp.4-6.

Improving Transfer of Agricultural Information, January 1998, Extension Digest, *MANAGE*, Vol. 5. No. 4 pp. 1-5.

Satyanarayana Patnaik and Daljit Singh Bedi, 2000. Information Technology in India, *Employment News*, 25-31, March 2000, pp.1 -3.

SECTION IV : TECHNOLOGY UTILIZATION

24

PEOPLE'S PLANNING PROGRAMME
A Brave Step towards Modernisation

— *Jayasree Krishnankutty* and *K.J Sherin*

Since 1996 the People's Planning Programme has been the flagship programme of the Government of Kerala. The State has outrun any other State in the country in the process of bringing power to the people's hands. It is a step-by-step, bureaucratic process that involves change in implementation and controls mechanisms, change of roles to existing staff, widespread campaigning etc., the State government estimates that it has devolved 60 per cent of its work to the local bodies.

Primary evaluation reports of the programme revealed that participation of officials in the initial setup of grama sabhas was comparatively less, there was a general feeling that the role of officers was not well defined and that co-operation of officials is not really obtained. The bureaucracy is alleged to be nervous about power slipping out of its hand.

Agriculture is the main occupation of the villages. The agricultural officers have a key role in the formulation, development and implementation of agricultural projects in the Panchayats. At large, the job of the agricultural officer becomes unquestionably intertwined with the implementation of People's Planning Programme. Their opinion can mirror the impressions felt by other officials from the bureaucratic setup. The nature of their work calls for close-knit association with the rural folk who are the direct target group of the programmeme. Thus the study was taken up to get the pulse of the officials regarding the programme and the perception about the dimensions of the programme.

Methodology

Thrissur district was selected as the location for the study. From the 3 Blocks of the district, 15 agricultural officers each were selected randomly to form the sample. To assess their attitude, 10 Statements were arrived at after item analysis of 60 Statements using officers of the status of Assistant Directors and above as judges. The responses were obtained as a 5-point continuum. To examine their perception about the attributes of People's Planning Programme, they were presented with 8 attributes arrived at after careful review of relevant literature.

Results and Discussion

It can be generally deduced from Table 24.1 that the officers harbour a positive attitude about the programme. The differential note that arose from them is that political overpowering may dilute the very purpose of decentralised planning. Majority of the officers (62 %) opined that involvement of too many people may result in responsibility to none, instead of added responsibility. They also expressed that they feel helpless because of being pressurised from both sides. Perhaps this is a point which has gone unheeded by most of the administrators, people's representatives and evaluators. As the developmental programmes encourage more and more involvement of the people, so have they complicated the work of the agricultural officers who have the dual role at the People's Planning Programme and conventional bureaucratic hierarchy.

A similar sentiment is mirrored in the idea that, with the involvement of Panchayat the procedure for bringing governmental assistance to people has become more elaborate. Agricultural officers are the implementing officers and they used to serve as the direct link between the government and the people. Perhaps this difficulty encountered at the initial stages of implementation of developmental projects through the 3-tier system will get looked into in subsequent monitoring and evaluation of the programme.

Table 24.1 : Attitude of the Officers towards People's Planning Programme

(n=45)

Sl.	Statements	Agree%	Disagree%
1.	The system eliminates official redtapism bureaucratic tangles etc., which were part of the traditional system.	47.61	33.32
2.	The procedure for bringing governmental assistance to people has become more elaborate with the involvement of Panchayat.	71.42	9.52
3.	The officers are pressurized from both sides that they feel helpless.	61.90	28.57
4.	Some of the clauses for the vigilance over the activities of agricultural officers disheartening.	42.85	-
5.	The fact that projects are custom-made for each locality supersedes its negative aspects, if any.	61.90	19.04
6.	With the activities of *grama sabhas*, carrying out my official duties has become more easier.	28.57	61.90
7.	Involvement of too many people may result in responsibility to none, instead of added responsibility.	61.89	38.09
8.	Political overpowering dilutes the very purpose of decentralized planning.	57.13	9.52
9.	Since people get to involve in all stages of operation of a project, complaints and problems are reduced to the maximum.	-	-
10.	The fact that changes or modifications can be incorporated in any stage of operation of a project, is a definite advantage over the traditional system.	90.46	9.52

The element of *participation by people* was undoubtedly given the prime rank by almost all the respondents. The *accountability* in the sense that the system is accountable to the people of its area of jurisdiction came as second in importance, by way of number of officers who treated it as important. The next important attribute *uniformity* which indicate that while functions at each level should not be overlapping, they should compliment each other, was ranked next in importance. Majority of the officers also saw *role clarity* as an important attribute. Role clarity in the context of People's Planning indicates a clear perception by the various levels, of their roles in the developmental process.

Table 24.2 : Perception of respondents about the attributes of People's Planning Programme

Sl. No.	Attributes	Frequency of respondents (n=45)	% of respondents giving ranks 1to 4
1.	Autonomy	18	40
2.	Subsidiarity	14	31
3.	Role clarity	27	60
4.	Complementarity	32	71
5.	Uniformity	36	80
6.	People's participation	43	95
7.	Accountability	41	91
8.	Transparency	18	40

Contrary to the common apprehension that the bureaucracy in general finds the system a threat to their position, majority of officers endorsed the programme in some of its positive aspects. Aspects such as modifications can be incorporated at any stage of implementation of the project and that projects are custom-made for each locality are some of them.

Summary and Conclusion

The agricultural officers had generally a positive attitude towards the People's Planning Programme despite some of its drawbacks and difficulties experienced by them in different stages. People's participation, accountability, uniformity, complementarity and role clarity were considered as the most important attributes of the programme by the officers. In their opinion these attributes made the system stand apart and above the traditional bureaucratic set-up through which developmental schemes of the State government were solely being implemented so far.

25

GROUP MARKETING
A Tool for Modernisation of Agriculture

— *Shibu Sebastian, K.J. Sherin* and *Nambiar Sajini Balakrishnan*

Kerala being a consumer State, is dependant heavily on the neighbouring States for its requirement of vegetables. The annual production of vegetables in Kerala is only 2.5 lakh tonnes as against a demand of 81.4 lakh tonnes. In this scenario, the Government of Kerala in a joint venture with the assistance of EEC (European Economic Community) launched a novel programmeme called KHDP (Kerala Horticulture Development Programmeme) in the year 1993. The objective of this programmeme is to utilise the rich potentials of the State in the horticulture sector and to promote cultivation of fruits and vegetable crops in Kerala. Vegetables are cultivated in small holdings in Kerala.

The Kerala Horticulture Development Programmeme (KHDP) marketing strategy is called Group Marketing. About 15 Self Help Groups (SHGs) consisting 200 farmers join together to form a marketing unit. The produce are collected at the field centres (FCs). The FC is managed by a committee of farmers called Marketing Master Farmers (MMF). One of them acts as the convener of the committee. These field centres also have a bank account. A secretary is employed to maintain the FC books and salary for the secretary is paid by KHDP once a year. The marketing centres are popularly known as Swashraya Karshaka

Vipani (SKV). The information required for marketing is also available in Radio and newspapers like *Malayala Manorama, Mathrubhumi* etc. The marketing is done on Tuesdays and Fridays.

The support provided include:

- Analysis of market volumes and price to help the farmers in taking marketing decisions.
- Training to MMF to help them negotiate with the trader.
- Trade linkages to ensure traders reach the field centre nearby.
- Help for the field centre to open a retail counter in the nearby towns.
- Production, planning, to grow produce when the price of the produce is likely to be higher.
- Management support through KHDP field teams.

A study was conducted in Trichur district of Kerala. About 50 farmers representing one SHG each selected as the respondents. The farmers were asked open ended questions with respect to marketing and the different strategies adopted by KHDP.

The following discussions with farmers was summed up into the following points:

1. Farmers get the prevailing market price for their produce.
2. Absence of intermediaries.
3. Absence of union, labour problems, and associated high costs for loading and unloading.
4. The farmer's produce are never sent back,
5. Products are graded at the field centres and appropriate prices are given for the produce.
6. The farmers do the loading, unloading and transporting of the produce, so there is no involvement of a third person.
7. The produce are sold by open auction.
8. The auction is conducted by the committee selected by SHG members. Usually the master farmers guide the marketing activities.

9. The observer of KHDP, monitor marketing procedure, to avoid any malpractice during auctioning.
10. The farmers have gained confidence and have enhanced their bargaining power.
11. The marketing operations are very transparent and all farmers are aware of the different procedures.
12. Farmers receive information on prices, arrivals and other details collected from Kerala and about markets outside the State, form an invaluable database for farmers. Information is also obtained by Supply Co and Horti corp.
13. The presence of bulk produce in village areas has initiated traders to reach these centres and buy the produce
14. The farmers get high payment regularly.
15. Better total realization.
16. Availability of cash when the farmers need it most.
17. Overall reduction in cost, time and energy the farmers have to spend while carrying out the marketing activity individually.

26

PRODUCTION AND MARKETING CONSTRAINTS FACED BY FLOWER GROWERS

— *P.H. Yelpanekar* and *G.K. Sawant*

Maharashtra is an ideal State for cultivation of wide range of commercial floriculture crops. The hilly areas such as Mahabaleshwar, Nashik, Lonawala, Pune have wide scope for floriculture crops like roses, orchids, carnation and gladiolus etc. Considering all the benefits, the value of floriculture no doubt, is a boon to the farmers, but the flower growers were facing several problems which affected the rapid development of this important industry in the State.

Methodology

An attempt is made in this chapter to review constraints in production of flower crops from Nashik and Pune districts of Maharashtra. The major constraints observed were grouped as 1. Supply, 2. Economical, 3. Extension, 4. Technical, and 5. Marketing.

Results and Discussions

An attempt is made in this chapter to review the various researches carried out and generalize constraints faced by the flower growers from Nashik and Pune districts of Maharashtra.

Different constraints viz. supply, economical, technical, extension and marketing constraints were studied and presented in the following tables.

Table 26.1 : Distribution of the flower growers according to Supply Constraints

Sr. No.	Supply constraints	Gaikawad (1992)	Sakore (1997)	Kalbhor (1998)
	Unavailability of –			
1.	Healthy and guaranteed planting material in time	69	47	80
2.	Skilled labour in time	–	50	50
3.	Chemical and fertilizers in time	56	26	—
4.	Irrigation water	45	36	42
5.	Timely loans	—	—	—

From the Table 26.1, it was found that majority of the flower growers faced the constraints like, unavailability of healthy and guaranteed planting material in time and shortage of water followed by unavailability of skilled labour and chemicals in time. This constraint can be reduced by supplying the flower growers various inputs by co-operative societies in the locality.

Table 26.2 : Distribution of the flower growers according to Economic Constraints

Sr. No	Economic conatraints	Gaikawad (1992)	Sakore (1997)	Kalbhor (1998)
1.	High cost of planting material	—	—	50
2.	High cost of manures, fertilizers and other inputs	96	—	87
3.	High cost of chemicals	100	85	85
4.	High cost of packaging materials	—	—	8
5.	High cost of transportation	—	—	83

Among the economical constraints, high cost of chemicals and high cost of manures, fertilizers and other inputs were the major constraints reported by majority of the growers. These constraints can be reduced by supplying the flower growers with various inputs like manures, fertilizers and chemicals and packaging materials with subsidized rates.

Table 26.3 : Distribution of the flower growers according to Technical Constraints

Sr. No	Technical constraints	Gaikawad (1992)	Sakore (1997)	Kalbhor (1998)
	Lack of knowledge of –			
1.	Improved varieties	24	43	60
2.	Land selection	—	—	—
3.	Timety application of fertilizers	90	40	65
4.	Storage of tubers	—	—	88
5.	Planting method and soil	—	—	91
6.	Diseases and their control	56	40	81
7.	Pests and their conirol	56	40	80
8.	Packaging of flowers	—	50	32
9.	Exporting of flowers	—	90	92
10.	Proper harvesting stage of flowers	22	13	—

Among the technical constraints, lack of knowledge of – timely application of fertilizers, diseases, pests and their control, improved varieties, exporting of flowers and lack of knowledge of packaging of flowers were important constraints faced by the growers. However, these constraints can be reduced by supplying the growers with latest information of various technical matter by using different mass media.

Table 26.4 : Distribution of the flower growers according to Extension Constraints

Sr. No	Extension constraints	Gaikawad (1992)	Sakore (1997)	Kalbhor (1998)
1.	Inadequate visits of extension workers.	—	68	68
2.	Less knowledge of extension workers.	—	55	—
3.	Inadequate literature in local language.	—	42	54
4.	Visits are not organized to the Universities	—	55	—

Inadequate visits of extension workers, inadequate literature on cultivation of flowers in local language were some of the important extension constraints reported by the growers. Government should provide consultancy service to the flower growers to reduce these constraints.

Table 26.5 : Distribution of the flower growers according to Marketing Constraints

Sr. No.	Marketing constraints	Gaikawad (1992)	Sakore (1997)	Kalbhor (1998)
1.	High cost on packaging	—	80	—
2.	High cost of transportation	34	47	54
3.	Loss of flower quality during transportation	84	50	67
4.	Careless handling by the workers	—	53	—
5.	Lack of cold storage facilities	100	100	—
6.	Commission agents deduct more commission	87	100	100
7.	Fluctuating prices of flowers	90	100	83
8.	Low price in local markets	75	100	—
9.	Difficult procedure of export	—	76	—
10.	Difficult in selling remaining flowers after grading.	—	60	—

Marketing constraints were deciding factors of flower cultivation. Majority of the flower growers complained about high rates of commission agents, fluctuating prices of flowers, loss of flower quality during transportation, high cost on transportation, lack of cold storage facilities and low prices of flowers in the local markets were other important constraints reported by majority of the flower growers. To reduce these constraints, Government should fix standard rates for different flowers in the domestic markets. Processing industries should be set up in the localities to reduce post-harvest losses.

Conclusions

It was concluded that majority of the flower growers from Maharashtra faced supply, economic, technical, extension and marketing constraints. Commercial cultivation of flowers had better prospectus if these constraints were eliminated. The supply constraints can be reduced by supplying various inputs at proper time while economic constraints can be reduced by supplying various inputs with subsidised rates. Technical constraints can be reduced by supplying the growers with latest information in time while marketing constraints can be removed by proper organized efforts of government and growers. Government should formulate proper policy for the benefit of the growers to keep this business smelling.

REFERENCES

Gaikawad, S. S. 1992 . A study of flower growers from Nashik tahsil of Nashik district. M.Sc. (Agri.) thesis, MPKV, Rahuri.

Kalbhor, R.S. 1998. A study of adoption of recommended practices of tuberose cultivation by the farmers of Pune diatrict. M.Sc. (Agti.) thesis, MPKV, Rahuri.

Sakore,V. D. 1997. A study of rose growers in Pune district of Maharashtra M.Sc.(Agri.) thesis MPKV, Rahuri.

27

TECHNOLOGICAL GAP IN ADOPTION OF MUSHROOM CULTIVATION IN HARYANA

— *Sube Singh, P.S. Shehrawat* and *V.K. Makhija*

Mushroom, which is also known as fleshy fungi, attracted the attention of man since ancient times. Its cultivation becomes more important in the countries like India where density of population is more as compared to the available cultivated area because it requires very less area and abundant availability of agro-waste material which can be utilized for its cultivation. It contains protein contents twice as high as vegetables except legumes. Mushroom production is important not only from nutritional and medicinal point of view but for exports and recycling of agrowaste. Its culture does not require fertile land and, therefore, does not increase pressure on already over burdened cultivated area as it is cultivated indoors and in addition small floor area, the vertical space can also be utilized judiciously as Stated by Chadha and Sharma (1995)[2], Pathak *et al.* (1998)[4]. The most widely cultivated mushroom in India is Agaricus bisporus (white button mushroom).

As far as mushroom production is concerned, Haryana is the leading mushroom growing State of India which is mostly cultivated by seasonal growers. In Haryana State majority of the mushroom growers produce only white button mushroom (95%) and very few oyster mushroom (5%) of the total mushroom production in the

State as reported by Chadha and Sharma (1995)[2]. The productivity of mushroom in Haryana can further be increased if farmers adopt recommended technology. This can be done if the farmers are aware about the new technology. Therefore, extension workers should make efforts to transfer the latest technology at the farmer's level by using appropriate methods to make them aware and motivate them to adopt recommended practices and to minimize the technological gap. Keeping this view in mind, a study was undertaken to find out the technological gap in recommended mushroom cultivation practices and study their relationship with selected socio-psychological traits of the mushroom growers.

Materials and Method

The study was conducted in Sonepat district of Haryana State, which was selected purposively because of having the maximum number of seasonal mushroom growers. From this district two blocks having maximum mushroom production, namely, Sonepat and Ganaur were selected purposively. From these two blocks one village from each block, namely, Badhane having 90 mushroom growers from Sonepat and Khubru having 85 mushroom growers from Ganaur block were selected purposively because of having maximum mushroom growers in the villages. Finally 100 respondents (50 from each village) were selected randomly for the data collection. To measure the technological gap of mushroom growers they were asked to reply different questions, which were framed keeping in view all the recommended practices of mushroom cultivation. The correct answer was awarded a score of two, partially correct one and incorrect reply was given no score. The scores thus obtained under various aspects of mushroom cultivation practices were summed up both respondent-wise as well as component-wise. The weighted cumulative frequency method was followed for computing low, medium and high level of technological gap.

The selected recommendations were grouped into six aspects on the basis of their nature for the purpose of explaining the findings of the study on the technological gap in adoption of mushroom cultivation practices. These were strain/variety and time of cultivation, compost preparation, spawn and spawning, casing, cropping, harvesting and storage.

The technological gap in respect of different aspects of the technology were computed in percentage by the following formula:

Technological Gap Index = R–A/A × 100

where, R = maximum possible adoption score that a respondent could be awarded in respect of a given component of the technology.

A = score obtained by a respondent by virtue of his adoption of a given component of technology.

A suitable schedule consisting of various questions on the above mentioned practices was prepared to measure the adoption level of the farmers. A personal interview technique was used to collect the information.

Results and Discussion

Distribution of respondents on the basis of technological gap in adoption of mushroom cultivation.

All the respondents were classified into three categories i.e. having low level of technological gap (less than 25%), medium (between 25 and 30%) and high (above 30%) level of technological gap as shown in Table 27.1.

Table 27.1 : Distribution of respondents based on extent of technological gap in adoption of mushroom cultivation

Sr. No.	Category	Technological gap score	Ranged in percentage	Percentage of respondents
1.	Low	6-12	below 25	41
2.	Medium	13-14	25-30	32
3.	High	15-20	above 30	27

Mean Technological gap score = 12.44 (25.92%)
Score range = 6-20

The Table 27.1 shows that farmer's technological gap score ranged between 6 to 20 with a mean score of 12.44 which is equal to 25.92 per cent is certainly considerable and needs to be minimized by making extension efforts. The Table 27.1 also reveals that 41 per cent of the respondents fall in low category i.e., having a technological gap less than 25 per cent. About one-third (32%) of the respondents having medium level of technological gap (between 25 and 30%) and about one-fourth (27%) of the respondents having high level of technological gap (above 30%). These findings have also been supported by Bhatia (1991)[1] and Dass (1996)[6] in other crops. Thus it indicates that about 50 per cent of the respondents (57%) were having medium to high level of technological gap.

Extent of technological gap in adoption of different practices of mushroom cultivation by the respondents

The practice-wise analysis indicated in Table 27.2 that maximum (40%). Technological gap was observed in case of compost preparation because it involves a lengthy and complex process as reported by Chadha and Sharma (1995)[2], Pathak *et al.*(1998)[4] followed by casing mixture (29%). The minimum technological gap was found in case of spawn and spawning which may be the resultant of having higher knowledge and adoption level on this practice. The higher technological gap in case of compost preparation, casing, strain/variety and harvesting and storage may be due to the reasons that these practices require special skills and sufficient finances, lengthy and cumbersome process has also been reported by Chadha and Sharma (1995)[2] and Sarkar *et al.*(1995)[5]. It suggests that concerted efforts should be made to bridge this gap as compost preparation, casing and strain/variety plays a significant role in increasing the productivity. The possible reasons for higher technological gap in adoption of recommended practices by the respondents may be due to their inability to seek more information by less participation in extension activities, low level of socio-economic status and small land holding. These reasons for poor adoption by the respondents were also reported by Tiwari and Kapoor (1988)[7].

Table 27.2 : Extent of technological gap among respondents based on different practices of mushroom cultivation

Sr. No.	Practices	Maximum possible score	Mean techno-logical gap score	Mean score expressed in percentage
1.	Strain/variety and time of cultivation	4	1.1	27.50
2.	Compost preparation	12	4.8	40.00
3.	Spawn and Spawning	7	0.98	14.00
4.	Casing	5	1.45	29.00
5.	Cropping	11	1.69	15.36
6	Harvesting and storage	9	2.39	26.55
	Overall	48	12.44	25.92

Relationship between Farmer's Socio-psychological Traits and Technological Gap

The correlation coefficients ('r' values) were worked out to know the association between socio-psychological traits, such as, age, education, family education, socio-economic status, extension contact, mass media exposure, change proneness, risk orientation and fatalism-scienticism with the technological gap in adoption of mushroom cultivation. The results indicated in Table 27.3 revealed that out of 9 independent variables, 5 variables, namely, education, family education, socio-economic status, extension contact, and risk orientation had significant and negative association with the technological gap. It implies that technological gap of the respondents decreased with each unit of increase in their education, family education, socio-economic status, extension contact and risk orientation as reported by Bhatia (1991)[1] and Dass (1996)[3].

The Table 27.3 also shows that other independent variables, such as, age, mass media exposure, change proneness and fatalism-scienticism also had negative association with the technological gap but not to the extent of significant level. These results are in consonance with the observation of Bhatia (1991)[1], Singh *et al.* (1996)[6] and Dass (1996)[3] in some other studies also.

Table 27.3 : Correlation coefficients between Technological gap and socio-psychological traits

(n=100)

Sr. No.	Socio-psychological traits	'r' values
1.	Age	-0.0392
2.	Education	-0.3536*
3.	Family education	-0.2122*
4.	Socio-economic status	-0.2954*
5.	Extension contact	-0.2263*
6.	Mass media exposure	-0.0535
7.	Change proneness	-0.1575
8.	Risk orientation	-0.4812*
9.	Fatalism-scienticism	-0.0328

* Significant at 5 per cent level of significance.

Suggestions

To promote the adoption rate of mushroom cultivation and to minimize the technological gap, the following measures are suggested, such as, extension agencies should give more emphasis and conduct training specially on the practices which are complex in nature and required specialized skills, like compost preparation and sterilization of casing materials, the training should be given to farmers at the appropriate time and as per the convenience of the mushroom growers, timely loan should be provided to the mushroom growers at low interest rate, timely good quality inputs should be provided at the subsidized rates at the village/block level by the Government agencies, Government should install processing units for the mushroom to prepare some value added products so that the growers can get appropriate return of their produce and the extension workers should visit the mushroom houses/farms regularly to provide the technical know-how to the farmers to minimize the technological gap.

NOTES

1. Bhatia, Rajesh. 1991. Sugarcane cultivation: Technological gap and constraints. M.Sc. Thesis.(unpublished) COA,CCSHAU, Hisar-125004.
2. Chadha, K. L. and Sharma, S. R. 1995. *Advances in Horticulture*. Vol.13. Mushroom (K.L. Chadha and S. R. Sharma, eds.) *Mushroom Research in India: History, Infrastructure and Achievements*. pp. 1-33. Malhotra Publishing House, New Delhi-110 064, India.
3. Dass. R.1996. Sorghum production technology: Technological gap and constraints analysis with special references to Haryana. M.Sc. Thesis (unpublished) COA, CCSHAU, Hisar-125004.
4. Pathak,V. N.,Yadav, Nagendra and Gaur, Maneesha. 1998. *Mushroom Production and Processing Technology*. Published by Agro Botania. 4E, 176 J. N. Vyas Nagar, Bikaner-334 003, India.
5. Sarkar, B. B.; Bhattacharjee. A. K., Mukhopadhyay. K. K., Amar Dass and Chatterjee, N.G. 1995. Mushroom in Tripura Agric. *Extn. Rev.* 7(2): 27-31.
6. Singh, Bharat, Shehrawat, Pardip, S. and Sihag, Saroj. 1996. Technological Gap in the recommended cotton production practices. *Agric. Extn* Rev. 8 (2) : 24-25.
7. Tiwari, S.C. and Kapoor, Pankaj. 1988. *Mushroom Cultivation: An Economic Analysis*. Mittal Publications Delhi-110035, India.

28

ESTABLISHING FARMER ORGANIZATIONS
A Vital Role for Extension

— *A. Shaik Alauddin* and *S. Anand Kumar*

HISTORICAL PERSPECTIVE

Historically, extension has mainly involved technology transfer, with the Extension Personnel (EP) transferring knowledge from research stations to farmers by using individual, group and mass media methods. More recently, extension has been asked to play a "technology development role" by linking research with community group needs and helping to facilitate appropriate technology development. It is in the historical context that the government agencies developed and designed a policy framework to help rural people become organized so that the delivery of services could be channelled through the various types of farmer organizations or groups. Well meaning policies also provided blueprint structures for Farmer Organizations (FO) in the form of cooperatives and commodity organizations in order to provide various inputs, marketing, and educational services to the farmers.

FARMER ORGANIZATIONS

Farmer organizations can be grouped into two types: one is the community-based and resource-orientated organization; the other is the commodity-based and market-orientated organization.

Community-based, Resource-orientated Farmer Organisations

This type could be a village-level co-operative or association dealing with inputs needed by the members, the resource owners, to enhance the productivity of their businesses based on land, water or animals. These organizations are generally small, have well-defined geographical areas, and are predominantly concerned about inputs. However, the client group is highly diversified in terms of crops and commodities.

Commodity-based, Market-orientated Farmer Organizations

These organizations specialize in a single commodity and opt for value-added products, which have expanded markets. They are designated as output-dominated organizations. Not specific to any single community, they can obtain members from among the regional growers of that commodity who are interested in investing some share capital to acquire the most recent processing technology and professional manpower. These FOs are generally not small and have to operate in a competitive environment. Research, input supply, extension, credits, collection of produce, processing, and marketing are all integrated to maximize the returns on the investments of the members who invested in the collective enterprises. Several successful cases are found in India, such as Anand Milk and other dairy FOs.

However, each farmer organization will need to define its own BASE (Basic Activity Sustaining the Enterprise). In India, for that matter there is tremendous potential for expansion of commodity based FOs.

ROLE OF EXTENSION IN THE PRESENT CONTEXT

In the present context, targets for forming groups and farmer organizations were given to EP without training them properly in the theory and principles of community organization. EP did not have many skills and not much experience in the process of establishing these organizations.

However, because EP in many countries lack knowledge, skill and blueprint policies, and high targets, they resorted to shortcut methods to establish farmer organizations and groups. Many EP presented government policies in an over simplified way to rural communities, suggesting that unless they are organized into cooperatives or associations or groups, they will not get government subsidies or access to credit and technical services. As a result, several FOs were established overnight on paper. Many FOs remained active during the period that government subsidies were distributed, but did not actively create cooperatives or partnerships and mobilize local resources to help achieve agricultural development. Mostly, the elite of rural communities captured all of the services and resources, while the poor and women were left out or received little benefit. Very few attempts were made to develop the management capacities of FO leaders, their members, and EP. Community organization and facilitation skills were not part of staff training programmes.

ESTABLISHING FO: NEW APPROACH

The traditional approaches to organizing farmers and forming cooperatives need to be revised to meet the following development challenges of the twenty-first century.

- The increasing absolute and relative poverty in many countries.
- The degradation of natural resources such as soil, water, flora and fauna.
- The low involvement of women in agriculture and other development programmes.
- The poor health and education facilities in rural areas.
- The increasing socio-political unrest among the communities.

Step 1 : Understanding the Village Community

EP should enter the community with an open mind and understand the community structure. They must understand the community power structure, problems, and opportunities for development. Walking around and talking to key people can help ease their entry into the community. EP should also develop an understanding of the entire community, including the poor and marginal farmers and women.

Some of the techniques that can help to understand the community are using key informant techniques, participating in the community meeting and tea stalls, and walking around. Understanding the ownership of community resources and people's attitude, knowledge and skills in the development or agricultural production will help the VEW learn about the community. The VEW can also understand the situation in more depth by collecting both qualitative and quantitative information on the levels of income and productivity, costs of cultivation, post-harvest losses, output utilization, and the likelihood of making striking improvements to each of these factors.

Step 1 is crucial and cannot be done in a hurry. EP must spend some time (up to a month or so) to get the feel of the village community structure, politics, groups and past experience in FOs.

Step 2: Identifying Potential Leaders in the Community

The usual tendency is for the EP to talk to formal leaders and commercial sections of the community. By using the sociometry method they can identify potential leaders. However, it is also important to be sensitive to the leadership structures operating in that culture and to the knowledge and skills needed to be a successful leader of a farmer organization.

In some cultures, it is wise to search for and contact middle-aged leaders of the area who are not too young or too old. Preferably, they should come from better-off families, have social status and respect, and be from farming households. Case studies of leaders who have established farmer organizations show that these leaders initially made considerable sacrifices, experienced financial losses, and had to be supported by their families. These leaders also had to struggle and negotiate with bankers, bureaucrats, politicians, critics and others including their own farmer members (Seetharaman & Shingi, 1992). This family background and grooming helps these leaders to deal with situations which they will have to face with confidence and without being cowed. Leadership of a FO is not a job for a sincere but ordinary farmer.

Step 3: Talking to the Identified Leaders and Seeking Cooperation from Other Agencies

EP might talk to these leaders on general agricultural development and get ideas and information on FOs in the village. They might also seek cooperation from government agencies and especially from NGOs (if there are any in the area) to help establish FOs and support them in achieving success.

Does the community have a farmer organization? If not, is there a need for such an organization? If the community has a FO. What is its structure and history of performance? How could the FO play a role in village or community development? EP can canvass for ideas from the community and add their own ideas on the need for and the role of FOs in the entire process of broad-based agricultural development. They can explain how FOs in other communities helped them in development. It is important to provide facts and figures to convince potential leaders of the possibilities and approaches for increasing the income of a sizeable number of farmers and for contributing to the economic development of the region. Good FO leaders might also receive political advantages through satisfied farmers and people living in the region. The leaders' support should be secured and key people encouraged to consult among themselves about the pros and cons of forming FOs in the community.

Step 4: Helping Local Leaders to Call Community Meetings

EP can help enthusiastic local leaders to call for community meetings. Sometimes more than one meeting may be needed to discuss the need for and the role of FOs in agricultural development. FO leaders from neighbouring villages can be invited to speak at these meetings. Farmer-to-farmer information exchange helps them. Sometimes smaller meetings can be held for low resource (small and marginal) farmers and minority to serve their specific needs. There is no harm in having more than one FO in a village.

It is important that producers from all sectors in the village participate in these meetings because the success of an enterprise-based FO depends on the volume of raw material procured from member producers. Every small or big producer contributes to this volume. The volume itself is more important than the socioeconomic status of the supplier. Prospective members need to be convinced that everyone benefits in proportion to his or her contributions, not just the big farmers, as is widely perceived.

Step 5: Nominating Core Group Leaders to develop or establish the FO

From the community meetings, core group leaders are elected or nominated to design the FO with further community consultation. If leaders are elected or nominated, EP should consider the issues raised in step 2 when assessing each candidate for election or nomination.

In situations where it is more appropriate to appoint a leader, the search for a suitable person is critical and requires time and patience. It is also critical that the selected leader be involved in the search for a potential agro-based enterprise to act as a BASE (basic activity sustaining the enterprises) for economic development. This process requires time, patience, and interactive and intellectual inputs. The VEW can help the appointed FO leader in this process.

Step 6: Developing an Organizational Structure for the FO

The VEW can help the core group of leaders in developing an organizational structure for their farmer organization. In the past, the "blueprint" approach was taken without understanding the function that the FO's structure plays in its performance. Group discussions help to highlight the need for careful planning.

The core group leaders main goal is to understand the appropriate organizational structure, composition, and working rules for the efficient management of their farmer organization.

Stage 1: Leaders should secure the relevant guidelines of other FOs and study them carefully

An FO can be initiated by the government or by farmers and the community. If it is government initiated, the leaders should obtain copies of guidelines and rules. If it is community initiated, they should talk to other FOs and get their guidelines and constitution. The core group should study them carefully and discuss how they can fit into their community needs.

Stage 2: Leaders should then draw up a tentative organizational structure and working rules for their farmer organization

They should consider various models or types of organizations that serve their special needs for agricultural development and discuss them with other experienced leaders from that village or neighbouring villages. The structure should serve the functions. At this stage, the VEW should, as far as possible, play a passive role because the leaders are the ones who are building the FO, NGOs also may share their experience and help leaders to develop an organizational structure.

Step 7: Gearing up for Action

In this step, FOs examines their action plans and task groups are set up to mobilize human and financial resources.

Step 8: Implementing Selected Projects

The following process may be useful;

- Start implementing the selected project(s)
- Secure resources and allocate tasks.
- Develop a calendar of activities to achieve the goal.
- Develop monitoring processes for reflecting on events and activities regularly, either formally or informally.
- Ask committee members to meet to discuss actions periodically and report to general members regularly to keep them informed and involved.

Step 9: Monitoring and Evaluating the FO's Progress

Usually evaluation is done annually to meet formal requirements. But VEW's can encourage FOs reflect on their activities more frequently so that they learn and improve their management skills. They need to watch for people who want to take over the FOs for their self-interest. It is important to take action against any negative influences. These monitoring or reflection processes help strengthen FOs and avoid self-defeating problems. The success of the farmer organization can be evaluated by measuring the increase in the members' productivity, the increase in their net income, and the net reduction in the cost of cultivation due to bulk purchase of inputs by the organization. It is essential to conduct monitoring and periodic evaluations.

Emerging Roles for Extension Personnel

Keeping in view the above detailed process, several extension roles can be conceptualized to help rural communities get organized, but we will focus on two important roles.

Empowerment Role

The term empower means to enable, to allow or to permit and

can be viewed as both self-initiated and initiated by others. For EP, empowering is an act of helping communities to build, develop, and increase their power through cooperation, sharing, and working together.

The empowerment role can be a cornerstone of the new approach to extension. Extension personnel need to develop a new philosophy where their role is to help farmers and rural communities organize themselves and take charge (empowerment) of their growth and development. Telling adults what to do provokes reaction, but showing them triggers the imagination, involving them gives understanding, and empowering them leads to commitment and action (Chamala, 1990).

Community-organizing Role

Village extension workers must learn the principles of community-organizing and group management skills (Chamala & Mortiss, 1990) in order to help the community, especially the poor or weaker sections, to organize itself for development. Understanding the structures, by-laws, rules, and roles will help leaders to plan, implement, and monitor their programmes and to perform this new role effectively. Skills in conflict resolution, negotiation, and persuasive communication help EP to develop FO leaders and members.

CONCLUSION

The role of extension will vary with the role of the organization, the sectors in which the organization operators, the services offered, and the organizational form used. Care needs to be taken in selecting a person or group of people. Who will take the lead in establishing community based or commodity based farmer organizations. The person such as EP, needs to be acquainted with and convinced of how the FOs can be used to increase the income of small producers. It is important to help the interest to strong the FOs with win-win strategies. Helping them to see beyond petty politics and personal jealousies and to develop inclusive principles for development has to be at the top of the agenda of extension in the present scenario. More importantly, however is that for sustained development one has to faster the creation of active participation and self-reliant farmer organizations.

The benefits of aid-funded donor projects have thus often been short-lived, an no self-reliant capacity resting on permanent indigenous institution has been built up to sustain them, once a major investment period is past. Thus not only FOs are essential to reach the large mass of small farmers, but also to ensure that sustained local development that benefits the majority takes place.

REFERENCES

Burkey. S. (1993). *People first : A Guide to Self-Reliant Participatory Development.* London: zed Books.

Chamala. S. (1990). Establishing A Group: A Participative Action Model, *Working Together for Landcare: Group Management Skills and Strategies*, pp. 1338, Brisbane : Australian Academic Press.

Chamala, S., & Mortiss, P. (1990). *Working Together for Landcare: Group Management Skills and Strategies*, p. 368, Brisbane: Australian Academic Press.

Gupta,V.K & Gaikwad,V.R. (1986). *Guide to Management of Small Farmers' Cooperatives*, p. 172, New Delhi: Concept Publishing Company.

Seetharaman, S.P., & Shingi, P.M.(1992). *Agribusiness Cooperatives*, p. 210, ICA. Domust Trust, New Delhi: Oxford & IBH Publishing Company.

29

IDENTIFICATION OF INFORMATION SOURCES USED BY THE FRUIT GROWERS

— *Santashil Dhar* and *Ravinder Kaur*

The modernization of Indian agriculture in the 21st century would entail the necessity to modernize the extension machinery. New challenges and priorities would emerge besides the pertinent ones, broadening the horizon of extension activities and responsibilities, which, only a geared-up Extension machinery can cope up. New vistas should be established to reach out to the farmers and assist them in adopting modern agricultural technology. In this respect, the sources of information play an important role, being a strong influencing factor in the farm decision making process. Moreover, for providing necessary information to the farmers, it must be kept in mind, which sources of information the farmers use most. The judicious use of these target-specific sources for information dissemination can make extension activities more effective at lesser costs and minimum labour. Hence, the study was undertaken with the following objectives:

(i) To study selected socio-personal characteristics of the fruit growers.

(ii) To identify the sources from which the fruit growers get information regarding cultivation of fruit crops.

METHODOLOGY

Twenty-five per cent fruit growers each from the district of Ferozepur and Hoshiarpur formed the sample of this study. Only those fruit growers were considered who were growing fruit crops on a minimum of one acre land. An interview schedule was developed for the study. Socio-personal characteristics of fruit growers like age, educational qualification, experience of orchard farming, and area under fruit cultivation was studied. Sources of procuring seedling and planting materials and sources of information regarding cultivation of fruit crops were also studied. The interview scheduled was pre-tested in non-sampled area. The data was collected during the months of April and May, 2000 by personally interviewing the respondents at their respective homes or fields.

The data was analyzed using appropriate statistical tools.

RESULTS AND DISCUSSION

Personal Characteristics of Fruit Growers

Age

Thirty-eight per cent of the fruit growers were in the age-group of 40-50 years and 34 per cent belonged to the 30-40 years of age group. Twenty per cent and 8 per cent fruit growers were in the 26-30 and 50-58 years of age groups respectively. About three-fourth (72%) of the fruit growers were in the age-group of 30-50.

Educational Qualification

Nearly half of the respondents (44%) had educational qualification upto middle school, whereas 32, 20 and 4 per cent of fruit growers were matriculate, higher secondary pass and graduates or post-graduates, respectively. More than three-fourth (76%) of the fruit growers did not have educational qualification beyond matriculation. This may have far-reaching implication regarding the selection of proper channels to reach the fruit growers for dissemination of technical know-how.

Table 29.1 : Distribution of Fruit Growers according to Selected Socio-personal Characteristics *(n=50)*

Sl.No.	Parameters	Frequency	Percentage
1.	*Age (years):*		
	26-30	04	08.00
	30-40	17	34.00
	40-50	19	38.00
	50-58	10	20.00
2.	*Educational Qualification:*		
	Middle school	22	44.00
	Matriculation	16	32.00
	Higher secondary	10	20.00
	Graduation and above	02	04.00
3.	*Experience of Orchard farming (yrs):*		
	2-5	31	62.00
	5-10	16	32.00
	10-15	02	04.00
	15-19	01	02.00
4.	*Area under fruit cultivation (Acres):*		
	1-5	19	38.00
	5-9	16	32.00
	9-13	11	22.00
	13-17	04	08.00

Experience of Orchard Farming

A majority of the fruit growers (62%) had upto 5 years of experience in orchard farming. Only 38 per cent of fruit growers had more than 5 years of experience of orchard farming. Only 38 per cent of the fruit growers had more than 5 years experience of orchard farming. Hence, it can be observed that fruits being perennial crops, a significant portion of fruit growers have little experience regarding fruit growing. On the other hand it may also indicate that the efforts of the various agencies to promote fruit cultivation are bearing results, and more and more farmers are becoming increasingly interested in fruit crops.

Area under Fruit Cultivation

Thirty-eight per cent and 32 per cent of the fruit growers had 1-5 acres and 5-9 acres of land under fruit cultivation, respectively. Twenty-two and 8 per cent had 9-13 acres and 13-17 acres of area under fruit cultivation, respectively. This might reflect that most farmers, having little experience, are hesitant towards investing heavily on fruit cultivation. This might not prove to be beneficial in the long run because modern methods of cultivation of fruits are more capital intensive, and hence, it might stand in the way of rapid modernization and mechanization fruit cultivation. The Fall-out may be lesser productivity and uncompetitive price, which may further discourage the farmers from investing in fruit crops. Moreover, fruit growers may be less serious about a smaller orchard than a bigger one and it may be difficult for extension agencies to pursue them to adopt modern technologies.

Table 29.2 : Distribution of Respondents according to Sources of Procuring Seedling and Planting Material *(n=50)*

Sl.No.	Sources	Frequency	Percentage
1.	Self-maintained nursery	06	12.00
2.	Private nursery	33	66.00
3.	Department of Horticulture	11	22.00

Table 29.3 : Distribution of Respondents according to Sources of Information used *(n=50)*

Sl.No..	Sources	Frequency	Percentage	Rank
1.	Mass Media	02	04.00	7.5
2.	Fellow fruit-growers	13	26.00	1
3.	Department of Horticulture	11	22.00	2
4.	Own experience	03	06.00	5.5
5.	University (PAU)	03	06.00	5.5
6.	Fellow fruit-growers and private dealers	08	16.00	3
7.	Fellow fruit-growers and mass media	07	14.00	4
8.	Horticulture Department, Uni. (PAU) and Mass media	02	04.00	7.5
9.	Horticulture Department, Uni. (PAU) and Fellow fruit-growers	01	02.00	9

Sources of Procuring Seedling and Planting Material

A majority of fruit growers (66 %) procured seedlings of fruit crops from the private nurseries. Only 22 per cent obtained them from the Horticulture Department and 12 per cent fruit growers maintain their own nurseries. It was observed that fruit growers having bigger orchards maintained nurseries for their own use. Other fruit growers depended mainly on the private nurseries. The seedlings and planting materials supplied by the Horticulture Department were considered to be highly reliable by the fruit growers but the hindering factors were irregularity and insufficient availability of seedlings from the Horticulture Department. The fruit growers, depended upon the private nurseries because they could give ample supply, free consultancy services and they were prompt in taking action if any problem arose regarding the supplied seedlings.

Sources of Information regarding Cultivation of Fruit Crops

Twenty-six per cent of the fruit growers gather their required information from their 'fellow fruit growers', whereas 22 per cent depend on the 'Horticulture Department' for this purpose. Sixteen per cent consulted 'fellow fruit growers and private dealers'. Fourteen per cent consult 'fellow fruit growers and mass media'. Six per cent fruit growers depend on their own experiences only and the same percentage gather information from the 'University'. Four per cent and 2 per cent fruit growers reported their sources of information as 'mass media', 'Horticulture Department, University and mass media' and `Horticulture Department, University and fellow fruit growers' respectively.

The results show that 'fellow fruit growers' is the most popular source of information followed by 'Horticulture Department' and 'fellow fruit growers and private dealers' combination respectively This result may be of immense importance to the extension agencies who would be able to streamline their efforts along the more popular channels of information reception.

The data further revealed that the fruit growers who had more educational qualification tended to depend more on the Horticulture

Department, University and Mass Media as the sources of information regarding cultivation of fruit crops. The fruit growers having more experience showed an inclination towards depending on their experiences only. The fruit growers who had larger area under fruit cultivation also showed tendencies to gather information from Horticulture Department. University and Mass Media. This may be due to the fact that these fruit growers were generally rich and influential persons of their locality and had good contacts with the Departmental Staff or University experts. Being rich, they could also afford higher education and various audio, visual and audio-visual aids and were more familiar with mass media.

CONCLUSIONS AND SUGGESTIONS

It is imperative that the sources used more by the fruit growers should be explored more for future information dissemination and transfer of modern technology. It is in this respect that the emergence of 'fellow fruit-growers' as the most popular source of information bears special importance. It is understood that fruit-growers tend to do what other fruit-growers are doing or have done and have got satisfactory result. Hence, it can be suggested that different extensive activities like education, training, discussions, method demonstrations, result demonstrations, etc, be conducted in groups comprising of 'fellow fruit-growers'. Every fruit-grower will be encouraged by seeing and learning from his fellow fruit-growers, during the extension education or training sessions, and, more importantly, will continue to do so long after such sessions have ended. Each one of them would gather the courage to take more risks seeing his fellow fruit-growers. Thus, an atmosphere of collective confidence and mutual support would be built, which would go far in improving the information and technology reception by the fruit-growers.

Apart from this better quality of support services e.g. supply of seedlings and planting materials, should be provided. The extension machinery would have to shed its legacy of an irregular, erratic and unaccountable image and emerge as a responsible, reliable, knowledgeable, benevolent and supportive organization equipped with more effective modes of communication and technology dissemination, well-prepared to take on the challenges of the new millennium.

REFERENCES

Chitambar, J.B. (1997), *Introductory Rural Sociology*. pp 193-202, New Age International, New Delhi.

Sandhu, A.S. (1997), *Textbook on Agricultural Communication: Process and Methods*. pp 21-45, Oxford and IBH Publishing Co., New Delhi.

30

ADOPTION OF ANIMAL HUSBANDRY PRACTICES BY RURAL WOMEN OF HIMACHAL PRADESH

— *R.K. Kalra* and *B.S. Hansra*

In a country with a large vegetarian population, milk and milk products are highly valued for their nutritive quality. In India there is a wide gap between requirement and availability of milk. According to accepted nutritional standards, the per capita daily requirement of milk is 284 ml. However, the country's availability is only 110 ml.

Although there has been increase in milk production, the gap between milk requirement and its availability has widened due to a larger increase in human population. It is believed that the milk shortage can be overcome with the rearing of animals such as crossbred cows which are economic and capable of producing a minimum of 1800-2000 litres of milk per lactation by using improved animals husbandry practices.

Realizing the need of animal husbandry, special stress has been laid by the Himachal Government on animal husbandry programmeme for improving cattle wealth.

This programme is to help the rural women to increase their knowledge, improved their skill and expand opportunities to use available natural resources effectively. Still, there are some gaps between that is and what ought to be and this need to be investigated with the following specific objectives.

1. To study the opinion of rural women of the project area towards animal husbandry practices.
2. To measure the level of knowledge of rural women in the project area about animal husbandry practices.
3. To determine the extent of adoption of animal husbandry practices by the rural women covered under the project area.
4. To find out the reasons of non-adoption and partial adoption of animal husbandry practices by the rural women.

Research Methodology

The study was conducted in the area of Indo German Dhauladhar Project, District Kangra, H.P. A multistage stratified random sampling design was followed to select study area and the respondents. The Indo-German Dhauladhar Project area composed of 100 villages of Kangra district of Himachal Pradesh. These 100 villages were stratified into three categories according to the elevation of the area. From each strata six villages were selected by simple random sampling method. Thus the study was conducted in 18 villages of the project area. From each category of villages, 100 respondents were randomly selected on the basis of probability proportionate to the size of each village. Thus total sample from project group consisted of 300 respondents. A control group of 100 respondents was selected randomly from three different strata of elevation. In this way total sample constituted 400 respondents, 300 from project group and 100 from control group.

Construction of Scales and Test

In order to know the opinion of the respondents and to measure their level of adoption two scales were constructed with respect to animal husbandry practices. The coefficient of reliability and intrinsic validity of the opinion scale come to be 0.78 and 0.88 respectively and of adoption scale was 0.92 and 0.96 respectively (test-retest method). The knowledge test was also constructed and the item difficulty index and item discriminating index were found out. The difficulty, index and the discriminating index of the selected

Statements were ranged from 30 to 80 and .25 to .70 respectively. The reliability and instrinsic validity of the knowledge test were 0.81 and 0.90 respectively.

Operational Definitions of the Dependent Variables

1. Opinion

It is the reactions of the respondents towards recommended animal husbandry practices.

2. Knowledge

It has been operationalized as the knowledge gained by the rural women about recommended animal husbandry practices.

3. The Extent of Adoption

It is level of adoption/use of recommended practices of animal husbandry. It can be mathematically expressed as:

$$Y = P_1W_1 + P_2W_2 + P_3W_3 + \dots P_nW_n$$

where

Y = Extent of adoption of recommended animal husbandry practices.

P_1 to P_n = Practices recommended for animal husbandry.

W_1 to W_n = Weights assigned to the recommended practices in terms of their relative contribution.

Findings

A comparison has been made between the project group and control group to study the opinion, knowledge and level of adoption to find out the real impact of the animal husbandry programme.

Opinion

The respondents have been classified into three categories by using 3√F method viz. low, medium and high based on their opinion scores. It could be observed that project group differed from control group in low, medium and high opinion categories. It was found that majority of the respondents (57-67%) had high opinion scores in project as compared to minority of the respondents (9%) from control group. It could be revealed that maximum number of respondents from project group were in high and medium opinion categories, whereas majority of the respondents from control group were in medium and low opinion categories. The higher opinion scores in the project group might be due to the fact that the various facilities were provided by the project to promote animal husbandry and different new schemes were also introduced in the project which could help the women of the project area for their easy adoption, and as such, they had favourable opinion towards animal husbandry.

Knowledge

As far as the knowledge level of the respondents is concerned, it was found that three fourth of the respondents (75%) were in high knowledge category as compared to a few respondents (3%) from control group. Nearly one-fourth of the respondents of the project group (24.33%) and majority of the respondents from control group (69%) had medium knowledge scores. However, from project group, a negligible percentage of the respondents (0.67%) belonged to low knowledge category, and more than one- fourth of the respondents (28%) from control group belonged to this category.

Thus, it could be concluded that almost the whole group (99.33%) of the respondents from project group belonged to high and medium knowledge categories, whereas as many as (97%) of the respondents from control group had medium and low knowledge scores. May be that project had made special efforts in the field of animal husbandry by providing intensive training during village training camps and field visits at village level, it could increase the knowledge level of rural women. However, still there is a need for more efforts by the project to bring all the respondents at high level of knowledge.

The present findings were in conformity with the findings of Federal Ministry of Economic Cooperation (1986). Jain and

Table 30.1 : Distribution of the respondents according to their opinion, knowledge and extent of adoption scores towards recommended animal husbandry practices

Project group = 300
Control group = 100

Category	Opinion				Knowledge				Adoption			
	Project group		Control group		Project group		Control group		Project group		Control group	
	F	%	F	%	F	%	F	%	F	%	F	%
Low	25	8.33	28	28.00	2	0.67	28	28.00	113	37.67	62	62.00
Medium	102	34.00	63	63.00	73	24.33	69	69.00	130	43.33	25	25.00
High	173	57.67	9	9.00	225	75.00	3	3.00	38	12.67	0	0
Non-adopters	–	–	–	–	–	–	–	–	19	6.33	13	13.00
Mean scores	6.81	–	3.80	–	9.81	–	3.85	–	11.40	–	6.72	–
S.D.	2.58	–	3.04	–	1.58	–	1.47	–	6.25	–	4.46	–

‘t’ values : 20.76** 21.01** 6.47**

** Significant at 0.01 level

Parshad (1975) and Kanjla (1980) who reported that majority of the participants after training, obtained more than 50 per cent scores.

3. Adoption

The data in Table 30.1 further revealed that 6.33 per cent of the respondents from project group and 13 per cent from control group did not adopt animal husbandry practices as they were not having animals. Out of the remaining respondents 37.67 per cent, 43.33 per cent and 12.67 per cent belonged to low, medium and high adoption categories from project group as compared to 62 per cent, 25 per cent and zero per cent of the respondents from control group respectively. It could be concluded that more than 50 per cent of the respondents had medium and high adoption scores from the project group, whereas only 25 per cent of the respondents belonged to this category from control group. This difference might be due to the fact that the project had made special efforts by providing intensive training, provision of jersey-bulls at village level for breeding, promotion and strengthening of artificial insemination centres covered under the project area, arranging calf rallies and field visits at village level. Due to these provisions, the respondents of the project group had higher adoption than the adoption of control group.

Further the perusal of the data in Table 30.1 showed that the difference between the two groups were statistically tested with regard to opinion, knowledge and adoption by calculating 't' values, which were found to be significant at 0.01 level. It indicated that the project group had higher opinion, knowledge and adoption scores than control group. It might be inferred that the respondents of the project area were relatively more progressive as compared to the respondents outside the project area because of intensive extension approach of the project.

Reasons for Non-Adoption and Partial Adoption

Although adoption score of the project group is higher as compared to non-project group, yet it can be concluded that there is a vast scope for the adoption. An effort was made to know the reasons for non-adoption of certain animal husbandry practices. The responses received from the respondents have been presented in Table 30.2.

It was evident from Table 30.2 that "repeat breeding" emerged as the main reason for non-adoption of artificial insemination as indicated by 21 per cent and 36 per cent of the respondents from project group and control group respectively. As such fertility promotion campaign would have to be launched in the area of study. The data further revealed that 11.67 per cent, 2 per cent and 26.33 per cent of the respondents from project group and 33 per cent from control group pointed out "high cost of feed", "non-availability of feed" and "grazing problems" as the reasons for non-adoption and partial adoption of recommended feeding practices. The present findings of high cost of feed was in conformity with the findings of Knight and Balasubramaniam (1982) and Reddy and Reddy (1972) who indicated that high cost of feed appeared to be the most important reason attributed to partial and non-adoption of cattle feed.

It was also indicated from Table 30.2 that 21.67 per cent and 19.67 per cent of the respondents from project group and 27 per cent and 26 per cent of the respondents from control group Stated "lack of finances" and "insufficient space" as the reasons for non adoption and partial adoption of recommended housing structure. 'Shortage of green fodder' was mentioned as a problem more by the control group than by project group. Shortage of green fodder was mainly due to shortage of seed, water and land. Incompatability of religious values with "*Gosadan* programme" emerged as an important reason in both the groups for sending unproductive animals to *Gosadan*. For this educational efforts seemed to be an appropriate prescription.

Thus the "grazing problems" and "incompatibility or religious values" were found to be the most important reasons for non-adoption and partial adoption of animal husbandry practices.

Anyhow it can be concluded that development programmes can bring desirable changes in the adoption behaviour of people.

Table 30.2 : Reasons for non-adoption and prtial Adoption of Animal Husbandry Practices.

S.No. Reasons	Project Group n=300			Control Group n=100		
	F	%	Ranks	F	%	Ranks
I Breeding						
1. Repeat breeding	63	21.00	V	36	36.00	III
II Feeding Problems						
1. High cost of feed	35	11.67	IX	33	33.00	IV
2. Non availability of feed in time	6	2.00	X	12	12.00	VIII
3. Greazing problems	64	21.33	I	5	5.00	IX
III Housing problems						
1. Financial problems	65	21.67	IV	27	27.00	V
2. Insufficient space	59	18.67	VI	26	26.00	VI
IV Shortage of green fodder						
1. Shortage of good seed	37	12.33	VIII	38	38.00	2.5
2. Small piece of land	66	22.00	III	38	38.00	2.5
3. Irrigation problems	47	15.67	VIII	21	21.00	VII
V Problems of discarding unproductive animals						
1. Incompatibility of religious value with *Gosadan* programme	78	26.00	II	40	40.00	I

In order to improve the cattle wealth of the country and to increase the milk supply it is essential to start more and more animal development projects. But at the same time it has to be ensured that needed facilities such as health care, food, loan etc. may also be provided in order to facilitate the adoption.

31

IMPACT OF SELF-HELP GROUPS (SHGs) IN FRUIT AND VEGETABLE SECTOR OF KERALA

An Approach Paper

— *S. Mothilal Nehru* and *N.K. Jayachithra*

Kerala Horticulture Development Programme (KHDP), a joint venture of European Union (EU) and Government of Kerala (GoK) was launched in the year 1993, with the objective to improve the overall situation of commercial fruit and vegetable growers of Kerala by increasing and stabilising their income. The emphasis is on increase in production and productivity, reduction in cost of production and improving the marketing system. The functional unit of the organisation is Self Help Group (SHG), comprising 15-20 farmers, who voluntarily join together on "neighbourhood" principle. Around 10-15 SHGs join to form a Field Centre (FC), catering to the needs of 200-300 SHG member farmers. As on date, there are 34,000 SHG member farmers of around 1,600 SHGs in six Project Areas/ districts. Since 1997, KHDP is implementing its activities more successfully. The strategies and methodologies used for implementation have resulted in increases in yields and cultivated area, improved marketing and credit facilities and a reduction in production cost: all of which contribute to an increase in farmers income (Beintvelsen, *et.al.*, 2000, MTRM Report).

Salient Features of the Programmeme at SHG Level

- Through the concepts of Self Help Group (SHG), KHDP is promoting the importance of self reliance among the commercial fruit and vegetable growers of Kerala. Group cohesion and participation of each SHG member in the group activities are ensured.
- SHG also acts as a medium for farmers in identifying and prioritising their problems and finding out their own solutions through experimenting themselves.
- Preplanned activity calendar of SHGs, Common code of conduct for SHGs, Common code of conduct of SHG meetings and Common fund formation and utilising procedures are implemented.
- SHG members select three categories of Master Farmers (MFs) i.e. MF -Production, MF-Credit and MF- Marketing, who are trained to take up the lead role and facilitate other SHG members to implement group activities in their respective areas.
- Planned and systematic efforts will be taken up by the FC level AMs to develop SHGs from the formation stage upto the stabilisation stage through the strengthening stage utilising the master farmers in the respective areas. Later, all the SHG activities will be undertaken by SHG members under the leadership of Master Farmers. The KHDP official at the field centre level is only a facilitator so that the MFs and other group members shall gradually take up the activities independently to reach the self help stage.
- As on 30th September 2000, from the beginning of the Programme in 1993, around 1780 Farmer Trainings, 610 Master Farmer trainings, 190 Project Staff trainings, 35 Bankers workshop, 11 Seed Growers training and some specialised trainings for Resource persons, experts and other specific target groups who collaborate with KHDP's activities were organised. These training programmes enabled the stakeholders of the Programme to imbibe the spirit of

participation and team work.

- Need based sequential participatory SHG level training programmes are organised in which the trained Master Farmers act as resource persons and facilitators. Practical aspects like imparting skills, field visits and demonstrations are the main components in a SHG level training programme.

Participatory Credit Planning Sessions

In the SHG level group meetings, credit plans are prepared to assess the credit requirement of eligible farmers. This session will be attended by the MF-Credit of the SHG, SHG member farmers and AM in charge of the particular FC under which the SHG operates. Credit plan is signed by the respective farmers of the SHG applying for loans, the MF-Credit and the AM-FC concerned. This session will enable to confirm the identity and. the integrity of the farmers applying for loan in a SHG.

- Credit to lease land cultivation, a scale of finance which is higher than that of NABARD, loan upto Rs. 25,000 without collateral security and exemption from service area norms are special features of the credit package.
- Proper utilisation of credit and repayment of credit by SHG members are ensured through group pressure. MF-Credit will take up the lead role in joint inspection of field with bank officials and motivates the SHG members for speedy repayment of loans. Further this will enable group renewal of loans. The credit recovery percentage for the banks under KHDP credit package has been nearly 90% (and in some areas even 100 %), which has shattered the age old myth that farmers are not in the habit of repaying bank loans, particularly leased land cultivators. This is unbelievable, but KHDP has evidence to prove it without any exaggeration. Around 17,000 farmers – most of them cultivating in leased lands are receiving nearly Rs. 38 crores of bank loans.
- Development of farmer friendly technology using the farmer's wisdom/indegenous knowledge combined with the

knowledge of scientific community through the novel concept known as Participatory Technology Development (PTD) is unique in Indian Agricultural Research and Development.

- PTD trials/experiments are planned, designed, implemented, monitored, documented and evaluated by farmers in a group. The farmers who are interested in taking up the trials on the basis of outcome of the participatory problem analysis sessions are facilitated by MF-Production and KHDP official in laying out experiments and availing the inference from the trials. This helped a lot to develop positive attitude towards experimenting new things among farmers.

Peand Disease Surveillance Programme

P'Itrials are particularly focussing on Pest and Disease mgement, especially on environment friendly practices and low coroduction inputs.

- Around 80 group marketing centres (also known as Field Centres–FCs) with 200-300 participating farmers from 10-15 SHGs are engaged in the sale of the local produce. The FCs have enabled the farmers to enhance their bargaining power than that of their counterparts in traditional markets. The farmers selling through the FCs these days get nearly 70-80 per cent, of the final consumer's price through the farmer's group bargaining power.
- The Market Information Centre (MIC) of Marketing Unit of the Programmeme collects the wholesale and retail prices and arrival of all major fruits and vegetables from local and some out of State markets. Reports are prepared on the basis of data collected on every morning. It is sent to broadcast and print media. The weekly summary of data is provided to all FCs. As the FC convenors are provided with the market information, the farmers will be well prepared to bargain with traders for a remunerative price.
- There is a FC management committee comprising MF-Marketing of all the participating SHGs in a FC area from

whom a convenor, a coordinator and a treasurer will be nominated. The day to day FC accounting is the responsibility of a paid secretary (external person).The monthly auditing of FC is conducted by an external auditor.

- As a process of strengthening transfer of technology, intensive campaigns are organised for improved cultural and plant protection practices, organic farming, pest and disease management and credit recovery. The Assistant Managers are provided with sufficient campaign materials such as leaflets, posters etc. which has helped to create an awareness among SHG member farmers and to provide wide popularity for improved practices.
- KHDP model with its grass-root network of SHGs, MFs and FCs have significantly improved the agricultural extension services for farmers in areas of fruit and vegetable production and marketing. The MFs, therefore form a nodal link between farmers, the project staff and the markets.
- Participatory Rural Appraisal (PRA) tools have recently gained importance in KHDP for the application in FC based micro plan preparation.
- The PRA techniques are widely being appreciated at SHG levels, especially in SHG meetings, participatory training sessions and in problem analysis sessions.

Social Impact and Institutional Change in Kerala

There has been a substantial increase of 86% in the area under fruits and vegetables in the Programme area, new horticulture crops have been introduced and there is a transition in the project areas from paddy-coconut system to a paddy-coconut-horticulture system.

SHG member farmers reported an increase in their incomes due to higher yields, reduced costs and improved marketing. Two possible adverse impacts were identified: the recent increases in lease rates for land tend to be more than the inflation rate as the demand for the leased land increased; and the prices of some vegetables seem to have decreased because of increase in supply implying a strong price elasticity for some products.

The KHDP approach has unmasked several myths: credit to landless farmers is feasible and high repayment rates can be achieved; the organisation of farmers into Self Help Groups (SHGs) without political alignments can be done; and the active participation of farmers in field research which is called "Participatory Research" is possible.

The approach of KHDP to train Master Farmers, who in turn train other SHG members not only increases the knowledge and skills of the farmers but also contribute to more self confidence, especially when they increased their yields and incomes. Access to credit for landless farmers creates independence from middle men. Farmers have become free to sell their produce. Evidence shows that traders are willing to purchase the produce on the farmer's terms.

Participatory Research is an empowering project activity as the inputs of both farmers and professionals are in principle considered of equal importance. The experience of farmers that they are able to conduct and analyse horticultural trials, is of great value for their self-confidence. At the same time, the farmers do appreciate the group approach in problem analysis, solving processes and the opportunity of shared learning through SHGs.

SHG members reported that their social status within their community or village has increased. SHG membership also creates a bond between the members, who sometimes start to undertake community based development activities beyond the KHDP context such as road construction with voluntary labour (Bentvelson, *et al.* 2000, MTRM report).

Success Factors

The following approaches have contributed to the success and sustainability of the KHDP model :

- Full time officers in field working with a single line of command, carrying out specific systematic work.

- The concept of SHGs, MFs and FCs as a grass-root network for improving fruit and vegetable production and group marketing.
- No distribution of free handouts to farmers, which contributes to sustainability.
- Easy access to credit, especially for farmers with leased land (i.e. without land as collateral).
- Group marketing through FCs, increasing farmer's prices and reducing their costs, as well as reducing costs for traders while providing them fresher produce.
- Confidence building in farmers through the Master Farmer approach and particularly through training.
- Participatory approaches, in particular Participatory Technology Development (PTD).
- Qualified and well trained staff at all levels including dynamic leadership.

Constraints faced by the Programme

- Contractual system of appointment resulting in high staff turn over.
- Difficulty in eliminating the sediments of subsidised input oriented system for changing the mentality of farmers to get them oriented towards self help.
- Some farmers expect assistance in the form of subsidies and kinds as they were used to such assistance from Government agencies.
- The habit of writing off agricultural loans was a constraint in creating a proper repayment mentality.
- In technical areas Research & Development linkage with external institutions is not sound, which needs further strengthening.
- Changes in concepts, strategies and implementation arrangements causing delays but eventually resulted in a successful KHDP model.
- Delays in approval procedures, transferring funds and land acquisition

Conclusion

KHDP is the single most organisation in India which could address both production as well as marketing problems of a very scattered and unorganised section of marginal and small farmers in the Fruit and Vegetable sector. While looking back to the seven years of experience in organising SHGs and implementing farmer centred activities, it is certain that the KHDP model is replicable in Development context also with slight modifications. In the context of globalisation, where global players engaged in Research & Development have a strong hold in the markets,the registered FCs of KHDP can become competent to collaborate with such 'Giant' firms for acquiring improved agricultural inputs and services. At that stage, KHDP farmers will be able to discard the mentality of waiting for any subsidised external help and will be financially strong to pay for the inputs and services on their own.

REFERENCES

Bentvelsen, C, Samarasinghe, B. Chatterji, S. and Nanda, A; *Mid Term Review Mission* Report (2000), KHDP, Cochin p. 2; pp 45-50.

KHDP (1995), *Self Help Groups in KHDP*, Kerala Horticulture Development Programmeme, Cochin, Kerala.

Seventh Work Plan April 2000- March 2001 (2000), Programme Directorate, KHDP, Cochin, pp. 18-74.

RECOMMENDATIONS

Based on the deliberations and interaction, the forum could bring out concert recommendations which are follows:

1. Joint research agenda can bring success for PTD and hence there is a need to link scientific and farming communities to facilitate Participatory Technology Development (PTD). While developing any technology, relative advantage, compatibility and complexity should be given importance.
2. An interdisciplinary team approach involving people and scientist need to be focused on the constraints of farmers in order to develop an effective research plan as people's planning has been found to be very effective.
3. Participatory variety selection can be adopted for successful technological development and the participatory methodology will be ideal for early spread and acceptance of new varieties. Further, planning may be done as an area specific programme rather than a general programme, in order to ensure co-operation of client system. People need to be involved in all stages of operation of the project concerned for success of the programme
4. Human resource development (HRD) should be given due importance in all the stages of technology development and its utilization.
5. Research system should address its research agenda according to the emerging needs of farming community and their economic status. Further, indigenous technologies should be blended with remote sensing and information technology and such advancements for better development of agriculture.

6. Some of the private seed production firms are found to have put-forth intensive extension effort in some areas, which can be made use of for the extension system may also give a helping hand wherever farmers are going to be benefited.

7. Suitable agro techniques should be developed and popularized among the medicinal plant cultivators as the present level of technology available is either inadequate or not disseminated properly. The indigenous knowledge on medicinal plants cultivation should be documented. Further Herbal gardens can be established in each agro climatic zone with all the locally available medicinal plants, to create awareness and acceptance among farmers. Bulk production of seed for large scale medicinal plants cultivation may be ensured.

8. Precision farming can be modified to suit local conditions prevailing in different areas. Suitable low cost technologies should be identified and can be modified to suit local condition and can be popularized among the farmers. More research on precision farming should be done for better adoption of precision farming practices. Farmers should be educated or trained on computer application, hi-tech agriculture etc. for effective implementation of precision agriculture.

9. For successful implementation of any crop improvement and other technology development programme through farmers participatory plant breeding, effective coordination and involvement of scientists, extension workers and farmers will be of immense use. Farmers should be directly involved from planning stage till the development, transfer and utilization of technologies. Further, feedback of technology generated and disseminated would be highly useful for further refinement and make them appropriate for larger area across the state or nation.

10. In the backdrop of emerging trends of privatization, the scope of exploiting private and corporate services in extension was effectively analysed. Pluralism in extension shall indeed mark the future of technology dissemination for meeting the ever changing needs.

11. Role of self help groups among fruit and vegetable growers in Kerala and few other States holds high promises of participative production and marketing to the great advantage of the growers and serving production interests of the country in a great way. This concept of SHG can be popularized in other places also.
12. Considerable measures are needed for creating awareness and achieving better utilization of labour saving low cost farm implements.
13. Services to farmers should be given through a single window system.
14. As generation of scientific information for field level application is a dynamic process, the need for continuous training and evaluation of the impact of training, etc, need special focus, to improve the efficiency of extension services.
15. Problems in the thrust-areas of different crop and farming system need to be analyzed with reference to rate of adoption. Proper information management system for different crops and farming system to be developed for further augmenting oilseed production.
16. New concepts like cyber extension hold good promise and are likely to dominate the extension scenario in the future and so deserves our attention.
17. The small and marginal farmers should be organized into SHGs so that they can market their produce by bulking it to make a good volume. This way these farmers will be able to trade, negotiate and bargain with the wholesalers to maximize their returns.
18. The experience gained by adopting a group approach for locally adaptable and sustainable agriculture in reducing the cost of cultivation of rice by applying 2 tons/ha. FYM and maintaining optimum plant population and low cost etc and getting a very high level of yield up-to 10.62 tons/ha should be replicated in the rice growing areas of the country where there is decline

in production, productivity and area.

19. To promote IPM technology, among farmers the bio-pesticides and the beneficial insects should be made available to them through an organized effort. Similarly, farmers and extension workers need training in identifying the beneficial bioagents and application of the IPM technology.

20. The adoption of farm machinery has been low. So efforts should be to make available the farmers the small energy efficient farm machinery and implements useful for different crops by giving subsidy if not to individuals than for farmers groups.

21. There is a need to develop entrepreneurship among the professional graduates and extension personnel as well to inculcate innovativeness, achievement motivation, information sharing, risk taking and co-ordinating and leadership abilities required to the challenges in 21st century.

22. To develop dry land agriculture there should be emphasis on effective water harvesting, soil conservation, developing and maintaining common pastures and speedy implementation of the dry land agriculture projects supported with required infrastructure.

23. The ITKs practiced by farmers need scientific analysis, documentation, screening, testing and validation by multidisciplinary teams. There is an urgent need for establishing a national body on the subject.

24. The adoption pattern of cultivation practices has suggested that farmers need to be advised more on seed treatment, balanced fertilizer application and disease control. Further, the technologies advocated should be need based and appropriate, economically variable. Socially acceptable and eco-friendly. Utilization of farm technologies has been very low and there is dearth of women extension workers. So women based extension system should function separately to improve the adoption of technologies by farmwomen.

25. Genetic engineering for sustainable development and

environmental protection need.

26. Interactive demonstrations for dissemination of agricultural technologies as one of the policies.
27. Farmer forecasts regarding weather, input, market and other necessary information.
28. New strategies to reduce burden of extension workers/ promotion policies.
29. Encouragement of co-operative farming/contract farming.
30. Benefit sharing mechanisms to farmers like GATT (General Agreement on Tariff and Trade)
31. Increasing scope for new approaches like FSR/participatory approaches/farmers led participatory approaches instead of top-down approaches.

INDEX